BELIEVE
Unlock Your Faith in
GOD'S PROMISES

JESSE DUPLANTIS

JESSE DUPLANTIS MINISTRIES
Destrehan, LA

BELIEVE

BELIEVE. In that simple yet profound word lies your destiny and destination. What you believe is who you are. Who you are will always become evident by what you say. What you say reinforces what you believe, and that brings your belief into your life.

Unless otherwise identified, Scripture quotations are taken from the King James Version.

Scripture taken from the New King James Version®. Copyright © 1982 by Thomas Nelson. Used by permission. All rights reserved.

Scripture quotations taken from the Amplified® Bible (AMPC), Copyright © 1954, 1958, 1962, 1964, 1965, 1987 by The Lockman Foundation Used by permission. www.lockman.org.

Scripture quotations marked (NIV) are taken from the Holy Bible, New International Version®, NIV®. Copyright © 1973, 1978, 1984, 2011 by Biblica, Inc.™ Used by permission of Zondervan. All rights reserved worldwide.

BELIEVE: Unlock Your Faith in God's Promises
© Copyright 2024—Jesse Duplantis

Published by Jesse Duplantis
PO Box 1089
Destrehan, LA 70047
www.jdm.org

All rights reserved. No portion of this book may be reproduced, stored in a retrieval system, or transmitted in any form or by any means—electronic, mechanical, photocopy, recording, scanning, or other—except for brief quotations in critical reviews or articles, without the prior written permission of the publisher.

Printed in the United States of America.

ISBN 13: 978-1-63416-438-2

BELIEVE

CONTENTS

CHAPTER 1
Have the Confidence to BELIEVE 7

CHAPTER 2
Mustard Seed FAITH...BELIEVE in Your Seed 13

CHAPTER 3
If God Said It, BELIEVE It 21

CHAPTER 4
Don't Shipwreck Your Faith 25

CHAPTER 5
Resist the Devil and BELIEVE 31

CHAPTER 6
You Better BELIEVE That You Have Benefits! 41

CHAPTER 7
BELIEVE and Do Not Be Moved 49

CHAPTER 8
BELIEVE in the Wonderfulness of Jesus 55

CHAPTER 9
BELIEVE Your Vision, Receive Your Dreams 63

CHAPTER 10
Success Is Believing God 69

CHAPTER 11
The Assurance of Knowing 73

Prayer of Salvation 81
About the Author 82
Other Books by Jesse Duplantis 83

CHAPTER 1
Have the Confidence to BELIEVE

Did you know that you can have full confidence in God and believe His Word? You never have to be afraid of expecting great things from Him. God loves you so much that He inspired 1 Corinthians 2:9 to be written, which says: *"…Eye hath not seen, nor ear heard, neither have entered into the heart of man, the things which God hath prepared for them that love Him."* God loves you, and His heart's desire is that you love Him and allow Him to move in your life and fill you with His confidence. The Bible says, *"…perfect love casteth out fear: because fear hath torment…"* (1 John 4:18). The world we live in is encompassed about with that disease called fear. I believe that Satan uses fear to either neutralize us or get us off on a tangent—and the purpose is to disarm us of the power we need to live out God's best plan for our life and the lives of people all around the world.

Fear is a disease that steals peace, kills joy, and destroys our mental acumen—it takes a sharp person and makes them unable to think with spiritual clarity or walk in truth. Fear makes a person look more at what Satan is saying and doing rather than at what God has already done and will continue to do. Fear can kill your belief in God and in His Word.

BELIEVE—He Is Doing a New Thing

I love the revivals of yesteryear. I've got books on the great revivals of the past, and I read them to glean as much as I can from them. They inspire me and show me God's habit of waking up and shaking up generations of people. I love it, but I don't live in it. I love what God did then, but I don't continue to try and revive those revivals of the past. Why? Because it won't change the future. You don't need revival… you just need to stay "vived!"

The apostle Paul said, *"…but this one thing I do, forgetting those things which are behind, and reaching forth unto those things which are before"* (Philippians 3:13). There is a future in front of us. God is doing a new thing today. What was back then was wonderful, but those revivals of the past won't meet the needs of the future. Why? Because that time has passed. God has already done that, and today He is going to move forward. *"Behold, I will do a new thing; now it shall spring forth; shall ye not know it? I will even make a way in the wilderness, and rivers in the desert"* (Isaiah 43:19).

That is why God wants us to walk with Him daily—not living according to past religious history…not living by the inspiration of yesterday. Not because what happened back then is wrong. It isn't. But because the inspiration of yesterday is not sufficient for today. How the Holy Spirit moved decades or centuries ago was wonderful, but the question is: How is God moving within your life today? You determine that, not Him. You have a daily obligation to believe the uncompromised Word of the Lord and allow the Holy One of Israel to use you.

Inspire yourself every day as you build yourself up in the Word. What does it say about you? Find out, let it sink in, and BELIEVE it. When you know who you are in Jesus, you can look at a lost, sin-sick world with hope. You won't see them as hopeless because you'll know that there is enough Jesus inside of you to reach out to them all.

That is why it is so crucial that you really believe what Ephesians 3:20 says. I want you to know in your heart that God is able to do "exceeding abundantly above all that you ask or think according to the power that works in you." Believe that and you'll have boldness and confidence to do God's will in your life.

For example, many years ago in South Africa, a man told me, "You've got more boldness than anybody I've ever seen in my life!" Confidence in who I am in Jesus gives me boldness. Why? Because

BELIEVE

I know that when I walk into a room, I'm the most powerful person there! When I walk into a place, especially if it's a heathen-ridden place, I am the most powerful individual around. Why do I feel like that? Because I know in Whom I believe. I know that my God is not just enough; He's too much!

Godly Confidence Makes the Devil Nervous

That kind of boldness and confidence makes the devil nervous. He'll say, "Watch that Jesse! Watch him!" I love to aggravate the devil! So, sometimes I start walking up to a person, like I'm going to talk to them, just to make the devil nervous. When I get close to them, I don't say anything and the devil looks like a fool. He gets all worked up over nothing and I think it's hysterical! He never knows what I'm going to do.

If you walk into a room and they are cursing, don't clam up. Do what I do and start praising! Man, I have walked into many cursing sessions. I love getting around people who curse because it gives me another opportunity to praise.

If you're a man and you've been to a gym where there is a men's dressing room or weight-lifting section, then you know how men can cuss! I don't know if it's the heavy weights or that there are just no women around to give men those disapproving looks, but it seems like when a bunch of guys get together, cuss words start flying.

One time, when they crank-started the cussin' motor, I stood right by them and started praising. It was so funny to see their faces. Their foreheads crinkled up and they said, "What? What?"

Then I repeated myself, "Praise God!"

"Praise God?"

"Yeah! Praise the Lord! Glory! Thank You, Jesus!"

Some backed away from me and made their way toward the far-off equipment. Others hung back and got quiet for a while, and then the questions began to come. And that is when I had the opportunity to let my light shine and tell them a little about my life serving Jesus.

There was one guy who spoke up and said something like, "I

Have the Confidence to Believe

don't believe in that blankety-blank-blank religious stuff!" That's when I got as bold as he was and said, "Well, glory to God, I do!"

I don't care about being confronted, and neither should you! Why? Because the Greater One is living in you! The Bible says, *"greater is He that is in you, than he that is in the world"* (1 John 4:4). As I said before, when I walk into a room, I'm the most powerful person there. I know it and the devil does, too! But that isn't so just because I'm bold. No matter who you are or how you are, if you're born again, then you're the most powerful person in the room. So, just BELIEVE that!

Now, sometimes you have to deal with people who want to push you around. They enjoy confronting you just for the shock value. They want to see your face or what you're going to say when they continue cussing and start talking bad about God. In those situations, I just do a little shock treatment myself. Instead of falling into a theological argument, I just give them simple truths from the Bible in a very matter-of-fact way. I don't argue. I just give it to them straight. If I'm talking about accepting Jesus in order to go to Heaven and they say, "Well, I don't believe in that," I just say, "That doesn't matter. Whether or not you choose to believe doesn't change the fact that it's true."

Then I start with the facts. "Look, you have two choices, Heaven or hell. That's it. There are no loopholes. If you say that you choose not to believe that there is a Heaven or a hell, then you're saying that you don't accept this Bible as truth and you're calling God a liar, which means that you also don't believe in His Son, Jesus. And your refusal to accept Him as your Savior is a choice that will send you to hell. But if you believe God's Word is truth and you choose to receive Jesus into your life, then you've made a choice that will send you to Heaven. So, Heaven or hell—which will it be?"

In my own experience, I've found that this kind of simple, no-nonsense approach works great with those who are confrontational and those who are into making up their own rules. I don't enter into any religious arguments. I just state the facts and ask them if they want to receive Jesus and go to Heaven. If they don't get saved right then and there, I know that at least they walk away having heard the truth. From then on, they'll be accountable for it.

BELIEVE

It Takes Courage to Have Confidence and *BELIEVE*

So, what will you believe for your future? Do you know? Have you prayed? Is it something that you can do on your own? Do you need His help? If so, I want to encourage you today that there is no such thing as "impossible" with God. What man cannot do, God *can* do and *will* do if you understand the power behind belief.

It takes a lot of courage to have confidence—and sometimes you have to tell yourself what you are going to do. Doubting is about going back and forth. It's about wavering. Faith is about standing firm in your belief and, after doing all that you know to do, simply continuing to stand and believe.

There are two portions of a scripture passage that I think we all need to really "hear" with our ears of faith. They are, *"Be strong and of a good courage"* and *"Only be thou strong and very courageous"* from Joshua 1:6-7. Notice the word "be" and realize that this is something *you* do. God cannot be strong and courageous for you. You must realize that He is with you, and because of that, you can "be strong" and "very courageous." How do you get to a place where you can rise up with courage? You do that by meditating on the Word of God. You must meditate on the Word of God because it is through God's Word that the full manifestation of what you believe will come to pass. This takes a lot of courage!

It takes courage to stand when everyone tells you that it's impossible. As for me, whenever someone tells me, "That's impossible," Hebrews 11:6 automatically comes up in my mind: *"But without faith it is impossible to please Him: for he that cometh to God must believe that He is, and that He is a rewarder of them that diligently seek Him."*

How is that verse able to pop up so quickly in my mind? How is it able to combat the naysayers of the world? It's because I take the time to sow the Word into my heart. You see, I know that I will be able to get *out* what I put *in*. I focus on God's Word and expect that the full manifestation of what I believe will come to pass.

Check Yourself Today:
Do You Have Confidence in God?

God will show you what to do and when to do it. He will anoint your every step. He will open doors no man can shut and shut doors no man can open. What is your responsibility? It is to simply believe and act on His Word. God wants you to be courageous—because it will take a lot of boldness to believe like this.

So, stir yourself up in the Word. "*...Faith comes by hearing, and hearing by the Word of God*" (Romans 10:17 NKJV). Never forget that your ability to BELIEVE is contingent upon how often you "hear" the Word of God—absorb it and implement it.

Check yourself today and shift your focus—because if you want to *have* what God said you can have and *do* what God said you can do, you must be dedicated to *believing* God's Word. Don't dismiss what He says just because it sounds impossible. God specializes in the "impossible," and as the Lord Jesus said in Mark 9:23, ALL things are possible to him who believes.

CHAPTER 2
Mustard Seed FAITH... BELIEVE in Your Seed

It takes faith to believe BIG! Faith is a divine design. It's God's idea, and His Son told us that we don't even need a lot of it to see results. In Matthew 17:20, Jesus said, *"If ye have faith as a grain of mustard seed..."* Now, notice how that is an extremely small amount of faith. Yet Jesus goes on to say in this verse that we can move huge "mountains" with just that small amount of true faith.

What does that tell you? Well, it tells *me* that even small faith can do big things! You see, when you have childlike faith in God's words—when you *believe*—your faith is given all the supporting assurances of God's almightiness and goodness. In other words, He causes faith to produce for you. Think about that for a minute!

God backs everything you believe from His Word with *Himself.* He is both the Author and the Finisher of your faith—it begins and ends in Him (Hebrews 12:2). God is the One Who makes His Word good. He is the One Who brings impossible things to pass. He is not limited by anything except by what He has already chosen to speak in His Word. So, if God said that even a small amount of faith, the size of a mustard seed, is what He accepts in exchange for His power to do the impossible, then He meant it and He will back it.

Think about the 30, 60, and 100-fold return that Jesus taught about in the parable of the sower. That is impossible math to unbelievers, but not to you. Why? Because you are a child of God and you BELIEVE! You know that it's your belief in His ability that actually brings the promises in His Word to pass no matter how impossible they seem. With God, nothing is impossible, and nothing is impossible for those who believe. Every good thing that you need, desire, and want in life will come as you consistently believe. Have faith in God and start thinking higher!

I want to take you to a very familiar verse of scripture found in Mark 9:23. There, Jesus says, *"If thou canst believe, all things are possible to him that believeth."* You could spend your whole life dealing with just that one verse. The key to total success in life is really boiled down to these two words: *BELIEVE GOD.* Whatever you need or want that seems impossible—whether it's spiritual, physical, financial, or in any other realm of life—you need a strong knowing and unified belief in order to see it come to pass. So, let's deal with the emotions that come up when you are stretching yourself to *believe God.*

Emotions—Turn Your Conflict into Faith

That verse, *"If thou canst believe, all things are possible to him that believeth,"* comes from a passage in scripture that talks about a father wanting his demon-possessed son to be delivered, healed, and at peace.

If you read the story, you'll see that the boy's father brought his son to Jesus' disciples, who tried but could not cast the demon out and free the boy. This shows you that when you follow Jesus, people will assume that His power is flowing through you, too. Don't forget that. It's important to have faith not just for yourself, but also for those who come across your path and need what you bring to the table of life.

When Jesus comes on the scene in this passage, everything changes rather suddenly, and His word of wisdom to the boy's father is simply this: *"If thou canst believe, all things are possible to him that believeth."* But look at what the man says in response in Mark 9:24. The man says, *"…with tears, 'Lord, I believe; help Thou mine unbelief.'"*

Emotions—I want to deal with them because, let's face it, *ALL* of us have been in the "Lord, I believe; help my unbelief" arena. So, how do we get out of this emotionally contradictory situation? We do that in two ways. One, by choosing to notice the difference between emotion and faith. And two, by deliberately choosing to SPEAK the future into existence by speaking the Word of God instead of just "telling it like it is" and talking about the present situation.

Never go to God with just emotional language. Go to God with what *He says* about something instead of what *you think* about something. What you think can change on a dime—because emotion doesn't confine itself strictly to one thing at a time. Emotion has a language of its own and can be tossed to and fro like waves on the sea. Why? Because emotion comes from the five physical senses.

Emotion *sees* something instead of *believes* something. Never go by what you *see*; go by what you *believe*. All your emotions do is tell you where you *are*—don't let them dictate where you go.

When Jesus says, *"If thou canst believe, all things are possible,"* then realize right then and there that there are NO limits on this promise. Let that sink into you now.

Your Seeds Create Blessings for More Than One Generation

Seed is the most valuable thing that we have. It is a tangible marker that helps us release strong faith. It jump-starts our mind and creates ripples in the spiritual realm. It starts for us the *moment* we don't hesitate to offer it in obedience to the Lord.

God keeps the books. God sees the heart. Whatever we do in sincerity to honor Him and whatever financial seeds we sow in faith create blessings that go beyond just us—they also touch our children. Blessings rest on the seeds of the righteous. Glory! The Psalmist David said it best: *"I was young and now I am old, yet I have never seen the righteous forsaken or their children begging bread"* (Psalm 37:25 NIV).

Did you get that? The harvest of the seeds of the righteous is for more than one generation! I really like the way Psalm 37:25 uses the word *never* in that verse—it means the seeds of the righteous have great power.

Between Seed Power and Active Faith, Nothing Is Impossible

Faith should never be idle. The Bible tells us in James 2:26, *"For as the body without the spirit is dead, so faith without works is dead also."* Don't let anyone kid you into thinking you don't have to *do* anything. Actions are important to increase your belief.

Between seed power and faith in action, *nothing* is impossible. Now, that's pretty simple, isn't it? It doesn't take much faith to get God's attention, and it doesn't take a lot to obey Him either. We all need to be more conscious of those spiritual facts.

Don't Waste Spiritual Energy on Difficult People— Never Mind Them!

Now, let's deal with the opinions of others. I want you to realize this: When you are doing something God told you to do, people will object—but just never mind them. That's a mouthful of truth right there!

There are some people who will always make things difficult by continually raising doubts and objections to whatever you are doing. Those who object and create difficulties are generally those who *do* the least and *give* the least. Never mind them! People may give you 101 reasons why you *shouldn't* do what God told you to do. Guess what? Never mind them!

Do you remember the story of the widow woman in 2 Kings 4, where the prophet Elisha gave that widow woman specific instructions on not only what to do, but also how to do it? Elisha told the widow to "shut the door behind you and your sons" in 2 Kings 4:4 for a reason. It was to separate her from the opinions of the crowd. Her miracle of the oil filling all the jars wouldn't have happened unless she had obeyed his command in faith.

It's easy to start worrying about what others may think when you're doing something out of the ordinary like using your faith. But your harvest is too important to allow the doubts of others to infect *your* faith. Safeguard yourself by "shutting the door," so to speak. If what they are saying goes against what God has said, never mind them! You are working on your future.

I'm sure you know what happened to the widow in this wonderful story. She was rewarded for her trust in the Lord, for her offering of a seed without hesitation, and for her obedience to act upon what the Lord was leading her to do in that situation. Every single jar was miraculously filled with oil—every single one! It was enough to pay the debt and save her children. Glory!

Recognize the Ones Questioning You

Faith and belief are tied up in the very essence of Who God is, yet so many people don't believe. I'm amazed at how many people there are who profess to be Christians who just will NOT believe the Word of God.

There are churches all over the world that think the Bible is really just a bunch of made-up stories, yet they have the gall to question people like you and me on our faith. They want to know what we believe and know concerning the Word and then question us—not so they can better learn to trust God and have faith in Him, but in order to better attack us for believing in the first place!

I like to follow the advice of Jesus concerning those kinds of questions—you can read it in Luke 23:1-9. When Jesus was brought before King Herod, He had already been mocked, blindfolded, beaten, and accused by both the chief priests and scribes. False accusations and questions were railed against Christ by the Sanhedrin—but notice that Jesus didn't waste His breath answering every little curiosity from people who had no intention of believing Him or freeing Him. To the Sanhedrin, He simply said (and I'm paraphrasing), "If I tell you, you will by no means believe. And if I also ask you, you will by no means answer Me or let Me go." In other words, He was saying, "It doesn't matter if I say a word or if I question you in return because your mind is already made up." So, Jesus stopped talking.

When they handed Jesus over to Pilate, the Word says that Pilate asked Him one question: Are you the King of the Jews? And Jesus, who knew that Pilate's intention wasn't just to trap Him, didn't elaborate on His answer. All He said was, "It is as you say" and, again, He stopped talking.

You see, Jesus understood that it is pointless to argue or answer fools whose hearts are already set. He didn't work to convince people who weren't really interested or open to God. When Pilate sent Jesus to face King Herod, Jesus immediately recognized that the king was really only intent on asking questions for the purpose of getting Him to do some miracle. And when Jesus saw his heart and "answered him nothing," the king immediately turned on Him, started mocking Him and treating Him with contempt, and sent Jesus straight back to Pilate.

Christ didn't fall into the trap of talking to people who didn't want to listen. King Herod couldn't get one word out of Jesus. Why? I believe that it's because, for years, Herod didn't care to hear Jesus' voice and he wasn't interested in truth, so Jesus didn't bother saying a word to him. He didn't let an earthly king force Him to speak, and so He simply chose not to say a word. I like how Jesus handled people—especially Herod.

You need to develop discernment in dealing with people who question your faith. If people want to criticize and say mean things about your beliefs, don't fall into the trap of immediately answering every foolish question that comes up. Be quiet. Recognize the difference between truly curious people and accusers. The more you stop and allow the Holy Spirit to guide you in everyday situations with people asking questions, the more you will develop a keen sense of the intentions of others when it comes to their questioning your faith.

Like Jesus, start noticing the spirit in which they are questioning you and, as necessary, choose to do what Jesus did with Herod—don't enter into the conversation. Don't even answer their questions. Remain at peace and don't fall into their trap. As 2 Timothy 2:23 NKJV says, *"But avoid foolish and ignorant disputes, knowing that they generate strife."*

God Wants to Bless You!

As long as people are carnally minded and fixated on doubt, they will not understand true spiritual belief—and your faith in

BELIEVE

God will never really make sense to them when they are in the natural. So, recognize that you aren't going to help anybody by arguing with them over faith.

Romans 8:6 says, *"For to be carnally minded is death; but to be spiritually minded is life and peace."* I believe with all my heart that unbelief is the chief reason for the Church's weakness today. It's a disease that manifests itself in many ways.

Being blessed is not about "deserving" or "not deserving." It's about the love and grace of God in action—a grace purchased by the blood of Jesus and blessings being shown to those who believe. This is what Jesus was telling that man about his possessed son: *"If thou canst believe, all things are possible to him that believeth."*

If you keep applying His Word to your life and BELIEVE, soon your mustard seed will flourish and produce orchards of blessings for generations!

CHAPTER 3
If God Said It, BELIEVE It

I really believe faith should be simple, so I'm going to make this as simple as I can. If a mustard seed can move a mountain, a teaching on how to BELIEVE God doesn't have to be complicated, right? OK! Are you ready? Three words: *"And God said…"*

You will find the words *"And God said…"* many times in the first chapter of Genesis. Notice that no matter what God said, it came to pass. So, what was the first thing God said? He said, *"Let there be light…"* (Genesis 1:3). After God said this, that same verse goes on to say, *"…and there was light."* In other words, if God said it, it happened—end of statement!

Throughout the Bible, if God spoke something, it happened. Guess what? Nothing has changed. Whatever God chooses to say happens. Jesus told us that every "jot and tittle" would come to pass (Matthew 5:18). God is serious about His Word.

So, let's go back to the very beginning, and let's think about His first words concerning this planet—*light*.

To Progress, You Need Light—*BELIEVE*

Light came first for a reason: there could be no progress without it. Darkness had to go for God's plan to begin. I like the word *light*—it is wonderful that God chose to do this first.

In every area, from the physical world to the spiritual, light brings clarity. Both physical and spiritual light gives your eyes something to *see*. Light was God's starting point from the very beginning. And when man lost his way, God sent His Son, Jesus,

Who was called "the Light of the world," to help us start again (John 8:12).

Light is always the starting point. Light is always the point of departure for our progress. If you want to progress in your life, you have to depart from where you are and start moving forward—toward light. Progress isn't going backward. Progress is always going forward. Even the physical light that God spoke into existence was not some philosophy to be debated or a problem to be solved. It was simply an illumination of His *will*. Light itself is still moving forward.

Now, God doesn't just throw words out there on a whim. God is purposeful, and light itself didn't just emanate from Him unconsciously—it was an act of His will.

God said, *"Let there be light,"* because He wanted light. So, His word was His will. He didn't say one thing but want another. This same principle applies to *everything* God says—including His Word to you and me.

So, what should we do when confronted with something God says? We should BELIEVE it.

Never Argue with God's Word—*BELIEVE*

I told you I would keep it simple! Never argue with God—just believe. Then, just do what He says. A debate makes it a discussion. A decision makes it a choice.

At some point, you have to make a decision about whether you are going to believe God's Word or not. I suggest believing. When you find yourself wanting to argue, just stop. Think about what you are believing for. Think about Who God is and remind yourself that everything He says comes to pass.

Remember that when God said, *"Let there be light,"* the light came into existence, and darkness left. You see, Jesus lives inside of you and He is the light of this world, so there should never be anymore darkness in what you do. If darkness tries to creep in, realize it and force it out with the "Light of the world" that resides inside of you.

BELIEVE

Refuse to Be Confused—*BELIEVE*

I believe that the cause of the world's trouble is the refusal to walk in the Light of Christ. That choice to dwell in darkness brings pain and sorrow to so many. Don't let the devil confuse you. God is not confused. His will is His Word—and He meant what He said. Satan is the author of confusion. Saint John said Jesus' life was the light of men (John 1:4). So, our job as believers is to *believe*.

How do we continually walk in clarity? We do it by keeping our faith ignited by listening to the scriptures. Faith comes by hearing God's Word (Romans 10:17). It's up to us to stay united with people of like precious faith in order to get rid of the confusion from the enemy.

Jesus made it His custom to go to church to hear the Word. It built His faith. He loved hearing and talking about God. We should try to be the same way—imitating Jesus like children. When we get up and leave church each week, we should take our faith with us and keep speaking faith day by day.

Realize that the Bible isn't just a bunch of stories; it's a living book. The words of God are in that book, and He says, *"My covenant will I not break, nor alter the thing that is gone out of My lips"* (Psalm 89:34). In other words, what God says, He will do!

You gain faith when you read the Word. You gain sound wisdom for living. These things are going to help you live well. So, when the devil tries to attack you and say you can't have what God says you can have, remind Him that God will not break His Word. There's nothing to argue about.

Quote the Word to yourself. Encourage yourself. There's enough discouragement in the world already; don't add to it by speaking words of doubt. If the devil attacks your mind with doubt, resist him. Shake it off and say, "No. God said it. He won't break His Word. I know my situation looks like I'll never have what God says, but I don't care what things look like. I know God's Word is true, and it will work for me!"

Some people say, "Well you never know what God's gonna do." That's not true. I know what He's going to do because I've read His book—and He's not double-minded or a liar. He is going to do exactly what His Word says. I know that I can be saved because Jesus said I could be saved—it's not open for discussion because God's Word can be relied upon!

Salvation is mine. The same thing is true with healing, prosperity, walking in love, and living in peace. All of God's promises and every fruit of the Spirit are available, just like salvation. Whatever it is, the only requirements are faith, patience, and obedience.

Do what He said.
Believe what He said. If God said it, BELIEVE it.
Have patience until you get what He said!

We've got to start looking at the things of God with simple, childlike faith because that's what works. Faith is a closed-book issue. The Bible tells us that the law came by Moses, but grace and truth came by Jesus (John 1:17).

Jesus came to the earth to preach, deliver, heal, and set free. Through His Word, we get wisdom and faith to live. Through His blood, we get access to God and eternal life. Through our belief in Him, we get the power to receive whatever we need. BELIEVE!

CHAPTER 4
Don't Shipwreck Your Faith

Have you ever faced a situation that threatened to shipwreck your faith? I'm talking about those times when your back is so far against the wall that there is no way to retreat. When you've lost everything you own, and it looks like you're going to lose your life. When it seems like what you're believing for must have been shipped to another address. That's exactly what happened to the apostle Paul. In Acts 27:1-10, he describes it in his own words:

> *And when it was determined that we should sail into Italy, they delivered Paul and certain other prisoners unto one named Julius, a centurion of Augustus' band.*
> *And entering into a ship of Adramyttium, we launched, meaning to sail by the coasts of Asia; one Aristarchus, a Macedonian of Thessalonica, being with us.*
> *And the next day we touched at Sidon. And Julius courteously entreated Paul, and gave him liberty to go unto his friends to refresh himself.*
> *And when we had launched from thence, we sailed under Cyprus, because the winds were contrary.*
> *And when we had sailed over the sea of Cilicia and Pamphylia, we came to Myra, a city of Lycia.*
> *And there the centurion found a ship of Alexandria sailing into Italy; and he put us therein.*
> *And when we had sailed slowly many days, and scarce were come over against Cnidus, the wind not suf-*

> *fering us, we sailed under Crete, over against Salmone;*
>
> *And, hardly passing it, came unto a place which is called The fair havens; nigh whereunto was the city of Lasea.*
>
> *Now when much time was spent, and when sailing was now dangerous, because the fast was now already past, Paul admonished them,*
>
> *And said unto them, Sirs, I perceive that this voyage will be with hurt and much damage, not only of the lading and ship, but also of our lives.*

Notice that Paul was very courteous when he warned them not to sail. An apostle of God warned them about what was going to happen. Whenever an apostle talks, you'd better listen. Yet the very next verse says, *"Nevertheless the centurion believed the master and the owner of the ship, more than those things which were spoken by Paul"* (v. 11). In other words, they had money on their minds. They wanted to get across the sea and sell their cargo, but they never made it. In verses 14-19, he goes on to say:

> *But not long after there arose against it a tempestuous wind, called Euroclydon.*
>
> *And when the ship was caught, and could not bear up into the wind, we let her drive.*
>
> *And running under a certain island which is called Clauda, we had much work to come by the boat:*
>
> *Which when they had taken up, they used helps, undergirding the ship; and, fearing lest they should fall into the quicksands, strake sail, and so were driven.*
>
> *And we being exceedingly tossed with a tempest, the next day they lightened the ship;*
>
> *And the third day we cast out with our own hands the tackling of the ship.*

Tossed with the Tempest

What does it mean to be *tossed with the tempest*? It means seasick! The deck of the ship was littered with food they had eaten four days earlier. They lightened the ship all right! Then they threw the cargo overboard. Paul could have said, "Idiots! Fools! Why didn't you listen to me?" Instead, in verses 20-25, we know that Paul encouraged them to believe God's Word:

> *And when neither sun nor stars in many days appeared, and no small tempest lay on us, all hope that we should be saved was then taken away.*
>
> *But after long abstinence Paul stood forth in the midst of them, and said, Sirs, ye should have hearkened unto me, and not have loosed from Crete, and to have gained this harm and loss.*
>
> *And now I exhort you to be of good cheer: for there shall be no loss of any man's life among you, but of the ship.*
>
> *For there stood by me this night the angel of God, whose I am, and whom I serve,*
>
> *Saying, Fear not, Paul; thou must be brought before Caesar: and, lo, God hath given thee all them that sail with thee.*
>
> *Wherefore, sirs, be of good cheer: for I believe God, that it shall be even as it was told me.*

It doesn't get much worse than this. They hadn't seen daylight for days, their cargo had been thrown overboard, and the ship was breaking apart. But I want you to focus on this last verse of scripture and never forget Paul's powerful words that were uttered to everyone on board that day. I think that they are three of the most profound words in the Bible: *"I believe God."*

I BELIEVE God

It didn't make any sense to believe like that because they'd already lost everything. But Paul wouldn't compromise what God had spoken. I want you to think about the word *compromise*. If you take away the first three letters, it spells *promise*. Paul had a promise from God, and he refused to doubt even in the face of overwhelming evidence that they would die. He was the only believer on board, but one believer can save everyone on the ship! I know that, because Paul's presence on that ship saved every life. I also know it from personal experience.

I was flying on a commercial airline, minding my own business and reading my Bible, when this guy looked at me and said, "Do you believe that?"

"Yeah!" I said.

He said, "I don't believe any of that book! I don't believe in your God. I don't believe in your Jesus!" except he was cussing the whole time he was saying it. I was so mad. I wanted to hit him, but the Lord wouldn't allow it. But let me tell you what happened next! Lightning hit one of the engines and it burst into flames as jet fuel spread to the wings. We dropped from 37,000 feet to 15,000 feet within seconds.

That man who'd just cursed Him screamed, "Oh, God!"

I know I shouldn't have done it, but I couldn't help it. I said, "He doesn't exist, remember? Enjoy death, you lying dog!"

The captain announced, "Get ready for heavy flame and smoke!"

Everyone on board began screaming. Nobody screamed for Buddha. No one screamed for Muhammad. No one screamed for Hare Krishna. You know what I heard? *"JESUS!"*

I jumped out of my seat and shouted them down. "You'd better thank God I'm on this plane!" I yelled. "Because life and death are not in that engine. Life and death are not in this smoke. Life and death are in the power of my tongue! If you stick with me, we'll land and nobody will be hurt. My God is able, and if He is for me, who can be against me? I'm more than a conqueror, and this day God has given me this plane! Now, I command that demon of hell to get off this plane!"

You know what they said? "Okay!" "Amen!" "Amen!" God answered my prayer and brought us safely to the ground. Just like the apostle Paul didn't compromise, neither did I. So, if you are believing for your family or loved ones, you shouldn't compromise either.

"But Brother Jesse, you don't know how bad my husband is."

No, you don't know how good my God is!

You see, compromise means that you don't take what God says as final authority. Paul said, *"Wherefore, sirs, be of good cheer: for I believe God…."* Paul's mind was not conformed to the waves. He didn't deny their existence; he just denied their right to kill him if God said they couldn't. The waves couldn't whip Paul, and neither can any of the storms in your life if you'll just believe God.

Make God's Word your final authority. Simply BELIEVE God.

God Is Looking for Faith

All He's asking you to do is step out on faith. See, our fight is the fight *of* faith. The problem is that most people just fight faith. "I tried that faith stuff and it didn't work!" Well, then, you can't please God because He said, *"Now faith is the substance of things hoped for, the evidence of things not seen. For by it the elders obtained a good report"* (Hebrews 11:1-2). That means when you stand before God, there's going to be a report given to Him about you. So, when I believe God for impossible things, I stand on Psalm 89:34: *"My covenant will I not break, nor alter the thing that is gone out of My lips."* That verse tells me that if God says something, then He won't alter it. If He won't, then I won't either. I don't care if everybody thinks I'm the biggest fool in town! What He's looking for is faith. So, I simply BELIEVE God.

CHAPTER 5
Resist the Devil and BELIEVE

When I got saved and started reading the Bible, I was like a kid with an ice cream cone—bright-eyed and full of excitement for what I was about to enjoy. I would read a scripture and think, *Wow!* It would stir me up so much, sometimes to the point that some people around me thought I was a little crazy. On planes, I'd read about Creation in Genesis and get so excited that I'd turn to the person sitting next to me and start talking about it as if it had just happened.

Some people think living for God is boring, but I enjoy my Christianity. I'm not saved enough to be miserable. When I meet people who are, I think, *They just don't know the God I know.* They may be saved, but they just haven't gotten to know Jesus enough to see how *good* He really is. They're usually either still holding on to their old ways of doing things instead of letting their "new creature" develop and grow, or they've done something worse…they've allowed the God in them to fade to the point that they are slipping head-long back into darkness.

Staying on the fence is miserable, but living for God is not. I tell people, "When you understand the God I know, then you'll understand the joy I have." It's just that simple. People ask me, "Do you get sad?" I say, "I tried sad. I didn't like it. I tried broke. Boy, I got away from that real quick, too!" I've realized something: The Word of God *works.* All it takes is application—which is faith in God, sheer tenacity to never quit, and one of the most important parts: a daily decision to resist the devil.

I'm no different than you. The devil tries to throw doubting thoughts and problems my way, too. He pulls at my flesh. He appeals to my "old man" regularly. But I've made up my mind that I'm not going to cave to his temptations. I'm not going to assist him; I'm going to resist him! He may fight me tooth and nail, but I *will* resist and I *will* reinforce his defeat.

Use God's Strength to BELIEVE, Not Yours

God never told us to fight the devil in our own strength. No, God gave us victory over *all* the works of the enemy when He sent Jesus to the cross. He gave us the power to resist *all* temptation and remain victorious. So, we don't have to fight an enemy that's already been defeated. We just have to walk in our victory by continually enforcing Satan's defeat. This is something we have to do daily, because the flesh is alive and kicking every day.

How do I stand strong when the flesh rises up? I choose to live in God's strength instead of my own. In other words, I refuse to allow myself to dwell on what Satan is attacking me with. Instead, in my mind, I resist him by shifting my thoughts to what the Word says. That way I have something stronger to fight with. It's not my original thoughts that are going to successfully resist the devil; it's the eternal thoughts of the Creator, God.

So, when I'm being attacked, I ask myself, "What does God's Word say?" It's not about fighting the devil; it's about walking on him! You see, the devil is under our feet. We don't have to fight, beg, or plead for him to go. Instead, we can keep our self-respect and just do what James 4:7-8 says: *"Submit yourselves therefore to God. Resist the devil, and he will flee from you. Draw nigh to God, and He will draw nigh to you. Cleanse your hands, ye sinners; and purify your hearts, ye double minded."*

When you turn your thoughts to God's Word and when you choose to use His strength to fight the battles of the flesh, you are doing one thing: submitting. You are bowing your own will and your own flesh to the will of God, and that's a recipe for success. The only time we will ever lose is if we fight an enemy that's already defeated!

BELIEVE

A Divine Example of How to Resist the Devil

Jesus gave us one of the best examples of not fighting the devil in Luke chapter four. In this passage, Jesus goes into the wilderness to fast and pray for forty days. He isn't finished for more than a day before the devil shows up and starts tempting Him.

> *And Jesus being full of the Holy Ghost returned from Jordan, and was led by the Spirit into the wilderness,*
>
> *Being forty days tempted of the devil. And in those days He did eat nothing: and when they were ended, He afterward hungered.*
>
> *And the devil said unto Him, If Thou be the Son of God, command this stone that it be made bread.*
>
> *And Jesus answered him, saying, It is written, That man shall not live by bread alone, but by every word of God.*
>
> *And the devil, taking Him up into an high mountain, shewed unto Him all the kingdoms of the world in a moment of time.*
>
> *And the devil said unto Him, All this power will I give Thee, and the glory of them: for that is delivered unto me; and to whomsoever I will I give it.*
>
> *If Thou therefore wilt worship me, all shall be Thine.*
>
> *And Jesus answered and said unto him, Get thee behind Me, Satan: for it is written, Thou shalt worship the Lord thy God, and Him only shalt thou serve.*
>
> *And he brought Him to Jerusalem, and set Him on a pinnacle of the temple, and said unto Him, If Thou be the Son of God, cast Thyself down from hence:*
>
> *For it is written, He shall give His angels charge over Thee, to keep Thee:*
>
> *And in their hands they shall bear Thee up, lest at any time Thou dash thy foot against a stone.*
>
> *And Jesus answering said unto him, It is said, Thou shalt not tempt the Lord thy God.*

Resist the Devil and Believe

And when the devil had ended all the temptation, he departed from Him for a season.
Luke 4:1-13

Notice the words Satan used. He said, *"If Thou be the Son of God...."* The devil didn't know if Jesus was really God's Son! He got confused about it and wanted proof. What does that reveal to you? It shows you that Satan is an idiot! He's truly a flesh devil who is continuing to lose his mind when it comes to the things of God.

Temptation #1: The Fleshly Body

The devil is unscrupulous—the boy never fights fair. Notice that he waited until Jesus was weak with hunger to start tempting Him with food. What does that reveal to you? Temptation number one reveals that Satan works in the realm of the *flesh*.

Where are *you* weak? Never forget that the devil never attacks you where you are strong. He always chooses your weak spot. His aim is to tempt you with the very things he thinks you will fall for—and it will always be in the realm of the flesh. But he is easily confused and if we resist him, he will get out of town. Jesus proved that.

So, notice that he first asked Jesus for something that he could see—bread. The devil figured if Jesus could do that, then it would prove to him that He was the Man! Jesus didn't take the bait. He refused to use the power of God for His personal advantage.

Instead, Jesus chose to *resist* the temptation by saying, *"It is written...."* When He chose to use the Word, He proved to the devil that He was in submission to God more than His physical body—and that He would not perform a miracle to satisfy His fleshly body.

If you want to be able to resist temptation in your own life, figure out your weakness and crucify your flesh in that area. It's not hard to know where you're weak. It's likely the same problem that rears its head regularly, if not daily.

Paul gave us the solution to this problem when he said, *"I am crucified with Christ: nevertheless I live; yet not I, but Christ liveth in* me: and the life which I now live in the flesh I live by the faith of the Son of God, Who loved me, and gave Himself for me"* (Galatians 2:20).

How does Christ live through us? It begins when we accept Him as our Savior and shed the old creature we used to be. But we enforce that victory in our lives by daily submitting ourselves to what the Word says—in other words, by crucifying our flesh so that our spirit can reign supreme. Do that every day, not just on Sunday, and you'll see a big difference in your ability to resist the urge to fall into temptation.

When is it hard to resist? It's hard to resist when you haven't been making the Word a priority. Life is busy and there are a million things to take your attention and your time, but if you make God's Word the last thing on the list, guess what's going to happen when temptation arises? You'll be scrambling and will likely slip.

You see, you've got to have the Word *in* you if you want to be able to draw from it when temptation comes…and believe me, you will be tempted in one way or another! So, do yourself a favor and give your attention to the Word of God. Read it. Listen to it. Quote it to yourself. Discuss it with others. Do whatever you have to do to seed God's Word into your heart. After all, Jesus Himself needed to use the Word to fight off temptation. So, don't you think that you do, too? God's Word is your strength.

Temptation #2: The Lure of Earthly Glory

The next stop in Jesus' temptation story dealt with pride and glory. When the devil brought Jesus to the high mountain and showed Him all the kingdoms of the world in a moment of time, he was offering Jesus the opportunity to rule over the "glory" of the world. Look at what he offered to give Jesus: *"All this power will I give Thee, and the glory of them: for that is delivered unto me…."* What was he talking about? The devil was referring to Adam, who delivered his dominion in the earth over to Satan when he disobeyed God's command.

Also, notice that everything God made has the ability to produce. His creation—the earth and mankind—is still pulsing with glory, even though it's been twisted because of sin. However, not all glory that is on this earth is from God.

The devil offered something he knew Jesus wanted—a kingdom. In other words, he said, "Hey, are you looking for a kingdom? I've got a kingdom! Listen, all you've got to do is fall down and worship me. Nobody has to know anything. It'll just be between us. C'mon, it ain't personal; it's just business. I'm making you an offer you can't refuse." He wanted to form a silent partnership with Jesus—a "you scratch my back, I'll scratch yours" endeavor that would satisfy them both.

Jesus didn't even bother with that. He said, *"Get thee behind Me, Satan,"* and started to quote the scripture again: *"for it is written, Thou shalt worship the Lord thy God, and Him only shalt thou serve."* What does that tell you? Temptation number two shows you that Jesus would not accept a substitute for God's divine order. He would not associate with wickedness, even for the attainment of a good end.

Satan had a motive. He wanted to offer Jesus what God was going to give Him in the end—power and glory. Notice that the devil offered a substitute. It was a poor substitute, but it was coming a bit quicker! He tempted Jesus to speed things up by going through the back door in order to obtain false glory.

When you deal with unscrupulous people, don't be drawn in by their promises of glory or honor. Never associate yourself with them. They may promise to change your destiny, but if it isn't godly, it's not the best plan for your life. Be aware that they aren't doing something for you for free—they've got a motive. When you stick with God, you always win. His way, even if it takes longer, is the right way.

Never accept a substitute "kingdom." The devil will offer you all sorts of things to get you off track. He's looking for a way in, and if he can tap your pride, believe me, he will. Do what Jesus did. First, rebuke him. Put him in his rightful place, which is behind you. Then, quote the strengthening Word of God again and move on.

Temptation #3: The Desire to Prove Yourself

Now, this next temptation shows just how far the devil will go to make his offers seem all right. He noticed that Jesus quoted the scripture twice in a row, so he decided to do the same thing. The devil asked Jesus again for a display of power. He asked Jesus to jump off the pinnacle of the temple, and he tried to make it seem reasonable by backing it up with this scripture: *"For it is written, He shall give His angels charge over thee, to keep thee."* This is deception, plain and simple.

The devil knew enough scripture to try to use it against the Son of God. What does that tell you? He knows the Word enough to use it on you, too. However, it will always be from a warped way of looking at things.

Notice that the devil looked for ways to find "common ground" with Jesus—to meet in the middle. He wanted to sound reasonable, but Jesus resisted. He refused to perform a godly act in a prideful spirit. Jesus refused to test God by jumping off the pinnacle of the temple. It was not a question of protection; it was a matter of honor.

Temptation number three shows that you should never perform a godly act in a prideful spirit. You don't need to prove yourself to the devil or people. Remember that even while Jesus hung on the cross, He was asked to do something prideful. When challenged to pull Himself off the cross to prove He was really the Son of God, Jesus didn't do it (Matthew 27:40). That was not His destiny and He didn't perform out of pride. Jesus understood the value of personal restraint.

So, notice this: The last step before falling is rationalization. Satan tried to make temptation "reasonable" in the mind of Christ, but Jesus wouldn't accept the rationalization. He stuck to the purity of the Word and did not use it to support His flesh. Instead, He used it to crucify His flesh. That's a big difference, and the sooner you get that, the less likely you are to slip into darkness.

This is about manipulation. The flesh wants appeasing, and the devil is a master manipulator. Don't be deceived into thinking that there is a middle ground. Most things in the Word are not gray areas; they are pretty black and white.

Jesus was powerful, so the devil tempted Him to *use* His power. But Jesus was wise enough to realize that just because He had power didn't mean He needed to perform like a circus monkey to prove it. Never fall into that trap. Do what Jesus did and stop foolishness right in its tracks. Hit the devil right between the eyes with the Word and go ahead and use the word "tempt" in your final blow to the devil, just like Jesus did.

After the last temptation from Satan, Jesus quoted this simple passage: *"It is said, Thou shalt not tempt the Lord thy God."* Jesus told the devil just Who was boss! In other words, "Don't tempt Me, devil. I'm God. You don't even have the right to do it." I love that! As a blood-bought child of God, you have been given all authority and power over the devil. So just as it was wrong for him to tempt Jesus, it is wrong for him to tempt you. God lives in you, so when he is attacking you, he is in essence attacking the God inside of you—trying to steal away the ultimate power.

He doesn't have that right, but he will try. When you peel away the actual temptation (in whatever form it takes) and you resist by using the Word, you are in essence saying what Jesus said: "Do not tempt me, devil. You don't have the right!" When you say that, you put him in his place. What will he do when he knows he's been beaten? He will do exactly what he always does: he'll give up for a while.

A Season Without Temptation

"And when the devil had ended all the temptation, he departed from Him for a season." For three months, the devil didn't bother Jesus. Why? He had experienced *resistance* instead of assistance! Jesus messed up his mind so badly, he had to go and rest himself. Notice that Jesus never squared off with the devil to fight. Why? He was more interested in what was going on *inside* of Himself instead of what was going on outside of Himself. Jesus knew that in times of temptation, you have to concentrate on your inner strength and what you know is right.

What did Jesus pull out of Himself? What did He use to resist the devil? I can't state it enough: He used the Word of God. That was His strength before the devil ever got there, and that's what He used when pressured. What are you supposed to use when the devil starts making you an offer you can't refuse? Again, the very same thing: you use the living Word of God.

This is a game to the devil—don't let him draw you into it. Don't start weighing the options and take his shortcuts. Remember that he is only trying to use and abuse you in order to hurt God.

If he appeals to the flesh of your body, you can resist. God doesn't want you bound by anything. He wants you free.

If he appeals to your desire for acceptance or glory and praise, you can resist. Let God lift you up instead. His glory and power do not come with strings attached, and they always come at the right time.

If he appeals to your desire to prove yourself to him, you can resist. You don't have to show the devil anything. You don't have to perform. The greatest performance that ever was has already happened. The cross won—end of story! You don't even have to fight—Jesus did that already. The devil is a liar and he is defeated, and he knows it. Now all you have to do is use the Word and *reinforce* his defeat.

You know what's right and wrong. Make your life simple by *resisting* the devil. Keep it short and sweet. Quote the Word, and don't budge no matter how appealing the temptation seems to be. The more you resist, the more irritated he will be. But then, like always, that fool will flee and *you* will be free…at least for a season!

Like I always say, the devil doesn't have any new tricks. He always uses the same old things to tempt you. Wise up to his ways. Focus on what's important—what God said—and stop fighting an enemy that's already been defeated. It is up to you to BELIEVE the promises of God so that you can walk in victory, free from Satan and his cohorts!

CHAPTER 6
You Better BELIEVE That You Have Benefits!

People ask me all the time why I'm so happy. Well, I'm simply exercising my benefits. I've made up my mind that I'm going to be healthy and I'm going to be happy. It's my right. I have benefits. I am a child of God, and I believe His promises.

Psalm 103:1-5 says, *"Bless the LORD, O my soul: and all that is within me, bless His holy name. Bless the LORD, O my soul, and forget not all His benefits: Who forgiveth all thine iniquities; who healeth all thy diseases; Who redeemeth thy life from destruction; who crowneth thee with lovingkindness and tender mercies; Who satisfieth thy mouth with good things; so that thy youth is renewed like the eagle's."*

I don't care what happens or how bad it gets; I care about how *good* it gets. I've had tragedy in my life and many, many problems, but I've decided that if God said I could overcome, then I will overcome. Problems aren't going to beat me; I'm going to beat them by the power of God that lives in me, and by the Word that He's given me to use. God's Word is like a sword against the problems of this world.

So, I'm not going to stop and build a house in the valley. No, I'm going *through* the valley! I am going to use my *benefits*…and one of the greatest and most important benefits of knowing God is being able to lean on His holy Word. In good times and in bad times, I will BLESS the Lord.

I've read many good books throughout my life, but there is no book like the Bible. The Word is living, breathing, decreeing, and

You Better BELIEVE That You Have Benefits!

declaring Who God *is* and what God *does*. It's filled with benefits that will empower you to prosper in every facet of your life—spiritually, physically, and financially. You can find out what God does in every book. From Genesis to Revelation, He is calling those things that be not as though they were. He's a faith God. He speaks and calls things into existence with the words of His mouth. That's what He does, and He wants us to do the same.

Who God *is* can be described by the fruit of the Spirit found in Galatians 5:22-23: *"But the fruit of the Spirit is love, joy, peace, longsuffering, gentleness, goodness, faith, meekness, temperance: against such there is no law."* These are His attributes that we are entitled to. They're the benefits of having the Spirit of God living and dwelling in us.

So, nobody can tell me that I'm going to lose my joy. My joy is founded in God, Who lives in me because of what Jesus did on the cross. No one has the power to take it away…nobody! So, I won't lose my joy, because *against such there is no law*. You can't take my faith either, because *against such there is no law*. And you sure can't steal my peace, because *against such there is no law*. Joy, faith, and peace are just part of Who God is *in* me, and I refuse to let someone else's misery steal it all away.

You've Got Something to Shout About

A lot of people think that emotion shouldn't be a part of a Christian's life, but I think otherwise. The Bible says that David danced, and that he danced with every fiber of his being in praise to God. In fact, the boy did it so strongly that the Bible says he danced his pants off (read 2 Samuel 6). He was standing around in his linen ephod (priestly garment), and his wife got mad about it.

Women don't like anybody seeing their husbands in their linen ephods! But David blessed (or empowered to prosper) the Lord with his dance. His heartfelt praise was seen by others and recorded in the Bible as a true display of one man's love for God. He was witnessing to others through that dance. He was acting out Psalm 103:1: *"Bless the Lord, O my soul, and all that is within me, bless His holy name."*

It's okay to get emotional about what you believe when it comes to the things of God. You get emotional when you care about something. People get emotional when they watch sports games or when they do what they enjoy. You often see players on TV who do their victory dances. Cathy and I talk about that, and we believe that it's good to show praise and joy about what you love and what you believe in. We've got God in our lives *and* His many benefits, and it's something to shout about!

So, if I'm believing God for something in my life, I don't act like I'm miserable even if I'm going through a battle. I choose to lean on a benefit. I choose to feel good. I choose to put God first—to reach people and change lives with His Word. I know that when I put God first and when I prosper Him, He will prosper me. Matthew 6:33 promises it: *"But seek ye first the kingdom of God, and His righteousness; and all these things shall be added unto you."* Notice it said the word "things"—God knows you need and want things, but He must be first before you can experience His prosperity.

Prosperity starts in the mind. It begins with blessing the Lord and filling your mind with His Word—His many benefits—so that you can prosper spiritually, physically, *and* financially. *"Bless the Lord, O my soul, and forget not all His benefits"* (Psalm 103:2).

Forgiveness for the "Twisted Stuff"

What are some of those benefits that we aren't supposed to forget? Forgiveness is one of them. Psalm 103:3 says, *"Who forgiveth all thine iniquities…."*

What is iniquity? It's all your twisted stuff—the issues that haven't yet become sin but are starting to cause you to twist or turn. It's things like, "I wish Sister So-and-So would leave this church. She's such an aggravating person. So, Lord, if You'd like to send her over somewhere else, please do so. I just don't like her, Lord." What kind of prayer is that? It's a twisted type of prayer. It's not right, yet there's no sin in it. It's just a person who's starting to twist. A few steps more and they'll be in offense, but right now, they're just starting to turn toward sin.

You Better BELIEVE That You Have Benefits!

It's also in gossip like, "Have you heard about…?" or "Don't tell anybody, but…." Gossip always comes camouflaged as a concern. This is a small example, but it shows you that God forgives you even before you dive headlong into sin. He *"forgiveth all thine iniquities,"* or twisted stuff.

Healing for All Thy Diseases

Here's another benefit of God. Psalm 103:3 continues and says that He is the One *"…Who healeth all thy diseases."* Now some people don't believe that, but either they are lying or God is lying…I pick them! God told us that He is not a man that He can lie in Numbers 23:19. It's impossible for Him to lie. Sometimes there are things that stand in the way and hinder our prayers, but healing is a part of God's benefit package and we should never dismiss it.

Too many people just accept sickness as a part of life and say, "Well, you know, Mama had diabetes, Daddy had diabetes, and Uncle Fred's hunting dogs had diabetes. Diabetes runs in our family. You know, our family usually ends up dying of diabetes."

If you ask them, "Do you have it?" they'll say, "No, no, but you know it's coming."

If you say, "Well, God will heal you," they'll interrupt you to say, "Well, I know, *but*…." That "but" really gets in the way! Yet God says He's the One *"Who forgiveth all thine iniquities; Who healeth all thy diseases."* These are His benefits, and they come when we bless the Lord with all our soul and everything that is within us, and when we bless His holy name and forget NOT His benefits. In other words, we have to remind ourselves of them so that we don't lose sight of God's power to prosper us.

Kindness, Mercy, and a Mouthful of Good

I'm always astounded by how many people I meet who tell me that they love me and are blessed by my preaching. People come up to me at church, in restaurants, and on the street just to say "hello" and let me know how much they love me. Why? It's not because of who I am. I believe it's because this scripture is at work in my life. I bless the Lord and forget not His benefits. Psalm 103:4 says He *"…crowneth thee with lovingkindness and tender mercies."* Isn't that wonderful?

At the very beginning of my ministry, the Lord said, "Jesse, if you'll stay humble and believe My Word and not hurt Me or steal from Me or hurt one of My flock, I'll cause people to fall in love with you." And that has happened. Now, I don't mean that arrogantly, it's simply the truth. I cross denominational barriers of every kind. I've preached in Baptist, Methodist, Episcopalian, Presbyterian, Church of God, Church of Christ, Word of Faith, Full Gospel, Assemblies of God, and even Catholic churches. I've also spoken in Jewish synagogues. When I tell them, "Don't you know I'm a Christian?" They say, "Yeah, but we like you." It's amazing to me!

I believe it is God's kindness and tender mercy on my life. Because, you see, I don't try to beat people up with my words. God never told me to beat people; He told me to lead people. Leaders in the faith aren't supposed to beat the sheep. We are to lead the sheep.

I'm not an "exposer" of people. I prefer to sow mercy. If you mess up, I don't say, "Well, you are a low-down dog from hell! No, I say, "Let's pray and ask God for grace and mercy in your life." Sowing and reaping still applies, and people may have to reap for what they've sown in this life, but God will always extend His hand of mercy toward them.

If you are out to judge and hurt people, they will scatter just to try to get away from you, and they will be no better off than before. But if you let the tender mercies and the lovingkindness of God flow through you, people will be attracted to the God in you, and then He can help them. What a benefit! The crown of lovingkindness and tender mercy is wonderful.

I love the next benefit in Psalm 103:5: *"Who satisfieth thy mouth with good things…"* The word "things" was added to make it flow, but the original says that your mouth will be satisfied with "good." To me, that means *good* ought to be coming out of your mouth. It is more satisfying to let good things roll off your tongue instead of bad things. Words of faith lift people up, including you. Words of doubt don't. Words of anger just breed more anger. Words of peace bring calmness. Life is more satisfying when good is coming out of people's mouths.

Youth Renewed Like the Eagle's

Cathy and I have been married now for 53 years, as of this writing, and not long ago she told me, "Jesse, you look better now than you did when I married you." I said, "Help her eyes, Jesus! I've got the photo album and it's just not true." When Cathy first saw me, I had a hard body…I'm talking muscles! I had abs that looked like they'd been cut with a razor, they were so tight. Well, I don't have a six-pack anymore, it's more like a keg, but that woman still thinks I'm something. Love is blind, and that's a benefit!

I've seen old people where the woman looked like she needed ironing and the man looked like a red pepperoni pizza had landed on his face. Yet, when they look at each other, they don't see that old age. They see an eighteen-year-old boy and a seventeen-year-old girl. Again, love is blind, and that's a benefit! But, you see, they didn't marry each other's body. They married each other. In her eyes, his youth was renewed. In his eyes, her youth was renewed, too. Isn't that wonderful? That's the power of love at work.

Nobody wants to age. Psalm 103:5 continues to say, *"…so that thy youth is renewed like the eagle's."* This entire passage of scripture is telling us that if we bless the Lord by putting Him first and winning souls (which is what makes Him wealthy), and we do not let His benefits escape our memory, He will renew our youth like the eagle's.

Have you ever seen an eagle's feathers? What color are they? Take a look at my picture and guess. That's right, silvery white!

It doesn't matter if you're going bald, you've got a keg for a stomach, and your wife's rear looks like it's been damaged by hail—if you both bless the Lord and forget not His benefits, you're going to get a divine overhaul! Renewed youth…and I'm not talking about cosmetically (although I do believe that what's in your heart is going to show up on your face); I'm talking about energy and strength to live well.

BELIEVE

I preach more than anyone I know. I'm constantly "going ye" with this Gospel of Jesus Christ, and do you know Who gives me the energy and the strength to do it? God. I consider energy a benefit of blessing the Lord with all my soul and keeping His benefits alive in my mind. That same energy is available to you, too. It's time for Christians to realize that they don't have to accept the problems and ways of the world. You and I have benefits, and we can put the Word of God on situations and see them change. Greater is He Who is in us than he who is in the world. If God is for us, who can be against us? We are more than conquerors, and no weapon formed against us is going to prosper. We have the benefit of God's Word and His presence in our lives when we simply BELIEVE.

CHAPTER 7
BELIEVE and Do Not Be Moved

The apostle Paul was a powerful preacher who traveled preaching the Gospel. Before Paul left Ephesus to go to Jerusalem, he wanted to be transparent and share his heart with the elders. In his farewell message to the leaders at Ephesus, Paul said some things that I want to share with you. I think they're profound and can change the way you live your life. His words sure have changed my life when it comes to BELIEVING God's Word!

> *And when they were come to him, he said unto them, Ye know, from the first day that I came into Asia, after what manner I have been with you at all seasons,*
> *Serving the L*ORD *with all humility of mind, and with many tears, and temptations, which befell me by the lying in wait of the Jews:*
> Acts 20:18-19

In other words, Paul was saying that he'd been with them through thick and thin. He'd been serving God with them and it hadn't always been easy. Paul wanted these men to know that he had to keep his mind humble through it all—meaning He had endeavored to focus on God's ways instead of his own ways. He wanted them to know that he'd shed many tears during this time and dealt with lots of temptation.

Paul also made sure to let them know that his mental struggles, tears, and temptations didn't come at the hand of God—they came at the hand of the Jews who were plotting against him. No, not the Romans. Not the heathens. It was those religious people who were trying to do him in! Sound familiar?

I can relate to Paul's problems with the religious crowd. In my ministry, I've had very few problems with the lost. They're more open and, sometimes, more kind! But I've had more than my fair share of problems with Christians. They backbite and criticize. They stir up all sorts of strife. They aren't just thorns in my flesh, they're complete bushes! How many times have I said to God, "It's those religious people, God. Wipe 'em out! They're messing up my witness and making it hard for me." But God doesn't listen to that. He loves everybody—even those Christians who irritate the socks off of me!

But Paul reminds his leaders that he never held anything back from them, even through the hard times.

> *And how I kept back nothing that was profitable unto you, but have shewed you, and have taught you publicly, and from house to house,*
> *Testifying both to the Jews, and also to the Greeks, repentance toward God, and faith toward our Lord Jesus Christ.*
>
> Acts 20:20-21

Paul led these elders by example, teaching publicly by going from house to house and witnessing for Christ. He was open and transparent with them. And as he travels back to Jerusalem, you can tell that Paul is feeling uncertain about what's going to happen to him. He says,

> *And now, behold, I go bound in the spirit unto Jerusalem, not knowing the things that shall befall me there.*
>
> Acts 20:22

Notice that Paul doesn't know everything just because he is the Apostle Paul. He's just going because he's under a commission from

God. But, even though he's uncertain about the future, there's one thing Paul is sure of:

> *Save that the Holy Ghost witnesseth in every city, saying that bonds and afflictions abide me.*
> Acts 20:23

Paul knew that he couldn't see results on his own. He knew the value and power of the Holy Spirit—that when he talked to somebody about Jesus, it wasn't his eloquent words that would make them consider salvation. Paul knew it was the pull of the Holy Spirit on their heart. He recognized that the Holy Spirit was witnessing with him through all that awaited him in Jerusalem—even tears, temptation, bonds, and afflictions.

Now, you'd think Paul would give up, right? I mean, it was tough for him to keep traveling and witnessing for Christ when the religious people were so bent on giving him a hard time. But Paul does no such thing. Instead, he sets his face like flint and says to the elders:

> ***But none of these things move me****, neither count I my life dear unto myself, so that I might finish my course with joy, and the ministry, which I have received of the Lord Jesus, to testify the gospel of the grace of God.*
> Acts 20:24

The bottom line? Paul would not give up.

Wipe Your Eyes and BELIEVE for Joy

Life's tough, but unless you want to fall down and die over your troubles, it's time for you to get up, straighten up your mind, wipe your tears away, resist the temptation to quit, and say, "None of these things move me!"

I've had many opportunities to fail and give up in my life and my ministry, but I just didn't take any. Some people think that's arrogant. It's not. It's called confidence. I've got confidence in my God—He is more than able to finish the good work that He began in me (Philippians 1:6). The Holy Spirit is working with me. I am not alone.

Paul decided not to allow the problems of life and the attacks of religious people to move him off of his course. He chose to go on. He chose to finish his course and fulfill his ministry duties with joy.

Now, some people think that I don't have any problems because I am joyful. They're living in a dream world! Problems come, but I choose joy. I choose to give those problems to God. Is it easy? No. But I refuse to allow worry and anxiety to rob me of my peace and sleep, and I refuse to allow the trouble that is thrown at me to rob my joy. I can get angry, but I don't allow it to go to the point of sin.

I don't walk around in la-la land, but I do choose the path of faith, and that gives me great joy. It's by the grace of God and my choice to have faith in God's Word that I continue on my course with joy.

Trouble Comes, But Who Cares?

It doesn't matter what the devil is doing, it's what God says that matters. I tell him, "Devil, if it's a fight you want, then it's a fight you're going to get. Come on, boy! Leap, frog! I'm going to do some damage to you like you've never seen before!" What is my weapon? The Word. I speak the Word to him and it cuts him like a sword. I'm not afraid of him!

If the devil is attacking me, I realize that while it may be tempting to allow my mind to struggle day and night over the situation, I will resist that temptation and give the problem over to God. Why? Because none of these things move me! No mental struggles, no sadness, no temptation, bonds, or temporary afflictions are going to move me off of my course. The devil will not win. I will maintain my peace. I will maintain my joy. Why? Because God has already given me the victory through the blood of Jesus. Now I'm enforcing the devil's defeat with every situation I go through.

BELIEVE

> *Ye are of God, little children, and have overcome them: because greater is He that is in you, than he that is in the world.*
>
> 1 John 4:4

I'm God's kid, and so are you! The Greater One lives in you. The devil is not greater than God. Religious people aren't more powerful than God. Sickness isn't more powerful than God. Neither is debt. No problem can match the power of your God. So why allow these "things" to move you? Stand up like Paul and say, "None of these things move me!"

If God be for you, who can be against you? What can be against you? If you say to that mountain in your life, "Go!" then it has to go. Period. Don't allow trouble to move you. You move trouble! That's what Jesus was saying when He talked about the mountain (Matthew 17:20, 21:21, Mark 11:23). He was trying to show you that you are in control, not the devil. He can fight, yes, but if you resist and use your Sword, he isn't going to defeat you.

Your weapons are far better than the devil's. You're using God's weapons, not your own. Trouble comes—Jesus said it would in John 16:33: *"These things I have spoken unto you, that in Me ye might have peace. In the world ye shall have tribulation: but be of good cheer; I have overcome the world."*

In other words, keep your joy and stick to the Word for peace. Realize that in this world, trouble comes. But who cares? Rebuke it and go on. Be of good cheer because Jesus has already overcome the world's troubles. When you get a revelation of that, it'll change the way you live your everyday life. Your shoulders will go back and you won't slump over in misery. You won't wring your hands in worry. You'll realize that the Overcomer lives in you, and there's nothing He can't do!

A Mark of Character

It's a mark of character to not be easily moved. Feelings change all the time, but the Word doesn't change. The devil sends trouble, but it can't stand the test of time. Faith and patience always win. When you choose to not allow the things of life to move you, you're actually building character. It's not fun, but by standing on the Word and not buckling in the heat of battle, your character strengthens. God doesn't send trouble to strengthen you—the devil is the stealer, killer, and destroyer—but you will get stronger by standing on the Word and defeating him. That's a fact!

The devil talks a lot. He makes a big spectacle to try and wave defeat in your face and get you to buckle. He knows you have more power, but it's a mind game to him. He knows that if he can convince you that you're weak, then he's got you. Just remember that all he's got is a big mouth and a mind game—he's roaring *as* a lion seeking whom he may devour (1 Peter 5:8).

The devil's not a big, burly lion—he's a wannabe! He wanted to be God—he's not. He wants to defeat you—he won't. He's defeated, restricted, rejected, and awaiting confinement. You could say that he is just out on bail until the Lord throws him into the bottomless pit, and then it is over with.

So, BELIEVE that Satan is already defeated. BELIEVE that the Greater One lives in you and has already made you more than a conqueror. With God on your side, there is nothing you can't do! And with faith and confidence like that, you too will be able to say like Paul, "None of these things move me!"

CHAPTER 8
BELIEVE in the Wonderfulness of Jesus

If the Gospels tell us anything, they clearly reveal that the atmosphere Christ created was electric and with all manner of possibilities. There were no two days alike when the disciples walked with Jesus. He created excitement everywhere that He went. He astounded His generation by His teachings and by healing the sick, raising the dead, casting out devils, and feeding the multitudes. They discovered the wonderfulness of Jesus.

The atmosphere that you and I live in, because of the wonderfulness of Jesus, also has all manner of possibilities. The Word of God declares that we can do all things through Christ who strengthens us (Philippians 4:13). When we realize the wonderfulness of Jesus, we can stand on His Word, walk in His Spirit, believe His joy, flow in His gifts, and grow in His fruits.

God is amazing at night and astonishing in the morning. When you get up in the morning to pray, you can have a fresh astonishment of Jesus. Be thankful for another day to live for Jesus and show His wonderfulness to others. When you go to bed at night, you can lay your head down and have a new amazement that the life of God flowed out of you and gave you the power to kick the devil's brains out.

This is the mark of a true disciple of Christ, not just one who claims to be a Christian. You know the type. They very seldom go to church, they just belong to one. They know about God, but they don't know God.

Believe in the Wonderfulness of Jesus

The true disciple of Christ has discovered how wonderful He really is. They can't wait to get up each day because all manner of possibilities await them to share the wonderfulness of Jesus with someone else.

I am often told that I make it seem so easy to testify for Christ. Well, first of all, when I testify to others, I don't tell them about my affiliation. I don't tell them I'm a Catholic, a Baptist, a Methodist, or Assemblies of God. I just tell them about the wonderfulness of Jesus.

I discovered that if I show someone how wonderful Jesus really is, they will want to experience Him for themselves. You'll never get anybody saved by asking them how they were baptized, but sharing the wonderfulness of Jesus will get results.

Are you allowing the wonderfulness of Jesus to work through you? Are your neighbors glad they live near you? Or do they wish you would move out because you are producing religion instead of producing the wonderfulness of Jesus?

If you are born again, people should see the wonderfulness of Jesus in you. It doesn't matter what state the economy is in or what the oil companies are doing. Man shall not live by oil alone, but by every word that proceeds out of the mouth of God (Matthew 4:4, my paraphrase).

Sin is a great disturber. It's the constant troubler of the human heart. It casts down that which should be uppermost. Sin casts down your conscience, your reason, and your holy aspirations. But Christ secures the human soul to its right condition. He re-dresses, re-establishes, revolutionizes, and makes all things new.

When you first get saved, Jesus re-dresses you and makes all things new. As you study the Word of God, you are re-established. When you receive the baptism of the Holy Ghost with the evidence of speaking in tongues, you become revolutionized. You refuse to allow the devil to destroy you because you realize that Jesus is in you.

You may know someone who has listened to the devil and walked away from God. You may be wondering how this can happen. Well, sin is a disturber. Like I said, it messes up people's conscience, reasoning, and holy aspirations. But God wants to re-dress

BELIEVE

them, re-establish them, and revolutionize their life. The Bible says, *"If we confess our sins, He is faithful and just to forgive us our sins, and to cleanse us from all unrighteousness"* (1 John 1:9). So, not only will He forgive their sins because of their confession, but He will also cleanse them. Why? Because His name is wonderful!

We who are in Christ have been selected as members of the cabinet council of Heaven, to which even the most favorite angel of Heaven is not admitted. We rule with Jesus with omnipotent power, yet with lamb-like gentleness. He sent us forth to proclaim the Gospel, heal the sick, raise the dead, and cast out devils. His omnipotent power to do the works of Christ is available to every believer. However, we are not to rule with a bulldozer but with the gentleness of a lamb.

The Psalmist David wrote, *"What is man, that Thou art mindful of him? And the son of man, that Thou visitest him? For Thou hast made him a little lower than the angels, and hast crowned him with glory and honour. Thou madest him to have dominion over the works of Thy hands; Thou hast put all things under his feet"* (Psalm 8:4-6).

I've never heard Jesus tell an angel, "Go to the world and preach the Gospel to every creature, heal the sick, raise the dead, and cast out devils." He gave that high honor and calling to us—His body, the apple of His eye, His cabinet council, the redeemed of the Lord.

The cross, in the disciples' minds, meant total defeat. But the wonder of God shows us that the brightest jewels are found in the darkest places. The disciples said, "It's over. It's finished. Let's quit and go back fishing. Jesus used to be Wonderful, Counselor, the Mighty God, the Prince of Peace. But now He's dead." But the brightest jewel of redemption was about to be discovered in the darkest place: the cross.

The cross typified total defeat to the followers of Christ. He was hung between heaven and earth to die in the place called "Skull," the hill of Golgotha. He was totally rejected by society, the 5,000 that He fed, and the multitudes that were healed and delivered through Him.

Jesus' darkest moment began as the sins of the world were laid upon His back and His Father turned away from Him. In total

Believe in the Wonderfulness of Jesus

isolation, He cried, *"My God, my God, why hast Thou forsaken me?"* (Matthew 27:46)

The Bible says, *"Yet it pleased the LORD to bruise Him, He hath put Him to grief: when Thou shalt make His soul an offering for sin, He shall see His seed, He shall prolong His days, and the pleasure of the LORD shall prosper in His hand"* (Isaiah 53:10).

How can God say He was pleased to bruise Him? Because the brightest jewel was about to be reflected in the darkest place. Psalms 16 and 22 say, *'The bulls of Bashan have encircled me…'; 'Will you leave my soul in Hell? Will you let my body see corruption?'* (My paraphrase).

The devil must have told Jesus, "Hey, He doesn't like you anymore. He's left you. He's forsaken you, remember?"

Then, hell, paradise, and the underworld began to crack and move as God, the Father, declared that Jesus had paid the price for man's sin and raised His Son from the dead.

Jesus put off principalities and powers by making an open show of them. The Father did not allow Jesus' body to see corruption. He walked out of that place and set the captives free. Jesus walked into Heaven with all the saints and boldly proclaimed that man had become the righteousness of God.

Jesus—He Gives the Reason and the Solution

I touched on this story briefly in chapter two, but I want to dive into it a little deeper. One day, Jesus approached His disciples and found them arguing with scribes and a whole crowd of people. He asked what was going on and, suddenly, one man from the crowd answered Him. *"Teacher, I brought You my son, who has a mute spirit. And wherever it seizes him, it throws him down; he foams at the mouth, gnashes his teeth, and becomes rigid. So I spoke to Your disciples, that they should cast it out, but they could not"* (Mark 9:17-18 NKJV).

Jesus is completely exasperated. But instead of condemning anyone personally, he says this: *"O faithless generation, how long shall I be with you? How long shall I bear with you? Bring him to Me"* (Mark 9:19 NKJV). Isn't that interesting!?

BELIEVE

Jesus was frustrated with the *reason* the boy remained afflicted—and what was that reason? Faithlessness. You see, to Jesus, Who really understood the power of belief, it was the faithless mindset of that generation (including His disciples and everyone present) that hindered the boy's deliverance.

Now, the boy's father goes on to explain all of his son's problems, and he ends his explanation by telling Jesus, *"...if You can do anything, have compassion on us and help us"* (Mark 9:22 NKJV). Jesus doesn't agree with the man but, instead, brings correction to the man's thought process. What Jesus says next changes the boy's life forever. It just may change yours, too. *"Jesus said to him, if you can believe, all things are possible to him who believes"* (Mark 9:23 NKJV).

You see, sometimes our thoughts need to be *corrected* if we want our faith to be *perfected*. What Jesus said that day changed everything. That man rose up from a powerless mindset and started to take hold of a powerful mindset—clarity came and he left the "faithless generation" behind.

If you are endeavoring to follow the teachings of Jesus and if you want to live an overcoming life that gets results, the statement of truth that Jesus spoke is one that you need to *know*. It will revolutionize your life!

Jesus—He'll Help to Change Your Mindset

When Jesus said, *"...if you can believe, all things are possible to him who believes,"* the Word goes on to say, *"Immediately the father of the child cried out and said with tears, 'Lord, I believe; help my unbelief!'"* (Mark 9:23-24 NKJV).

Now some might say the boy's father was wavering, but to Jesus, he was not. He was *hearing* and in the midst of trying to change. What did Jesus take away from the boy's father? 1) A heartfelt confession of the belief in Jesus as his Lord. 2) A heartfelt request for more of exactly what Jesus was talking about—BELIEF.

You see, that man didn't passively listen to what Jesus said—he *heard*. And we know that *"Faith cometh by hearing, and hearing by the Word of God"* (Romans 10:17). Real belief doesn't come by arguing. It doesn't come by making excuses and sharpening the intellectual ability to doubt. Real belief comes by *hearing* the truth. The Word of God *is* the truth.

Why did Jesus bring correction? Because He wanted the man to have what he desired. He wanted the man to *know* that he had power—it was in what he could *believe.*

If that man had ignored the truth and continued to believe that all he needed was for Jesus to have compassion on his family, well, that boy would have remained in his state of affliction. The truth required change.

Jesus—His Truth Does Not Change

This boy and his father lived over two thousand years ago, but the truth that worked for them will still work for us today. The truth does not change. We serve the same Jesus, and He is the same *"yesterday, today, and forever"* (Hebrews 13:8). So, the very same thing that helped that family can help yours, too.

We live in a "faithless generation" like they lived in, but we can still get wonderful results if we are willing to stop arguing amongst ourselves, *hear* what Jesus has *said,* and respond to *truth.*

Think about exactly what you need and want from the Lord and start meditating on Mark 9:23: *"...if you can believe, all things are possible to him who believes."* What a powerful statement!

If you look at this story of the afflicted boy, you'll see that nothing happened until *truth* was spoken. Nothing happened until the boy's father *knew* it was the truth and responded. That's when Jesus brought the boy out of affliction and into a healthy state of being.

Never forget that it's not just the truth that will set you free; it's that *"...ye shall <u>know</u> the truth, and the truth shall make you free"* (John 8:32). So, what do you *know?* What have you *heard?* How are you *responding?* Hear the Word and endeavor to *know* it. It will be faithful to make you free no matter what you are facing.

Jesus—He'll Let You Use His Power

What was Jesus doing in Mark 9:23? He was laying down your future! It's amazing how much "future" you have in your mouth. If you search, you will see that Jesus often taught on the power of words—revelations that sometimes began with, *"If <u>you</u> would <u>say</u>..."*

When you take hold of true belief, you are using the power of Christ and His omnipotence. Now that's a big chunk of ability! It's beyond earthly and natural. That kind of belief is divine. All that God *is* and all that He forever *will be*, that's the power that's available to you, and you tap into it with your belief. The power of Jesus is in your faith. Isn't that wonderful!?

You see, when you *use* your belief and faith, you increase in power and you perpetuate your future successes. Why? Because you automatically acquire more faith when you use the faith you've got! That's why, as believers, we must strive to have ever-increasing belief and faith.

Jesus—Let Him Elevate You Today

Why did Jesus reverse that father's mindset? Because He wanted to elevate the man's thinking so that he could get results. Jesus wasn't trying to show off His personal abilities. He was trying to show the man and all of us who would read the passage in Mark 9 that WE have the ability to draw divine power into our everyday realities.

When your mind gets elevated with Christ's truth, it will take you to a place of actually being able to receive all the promises of God. The Bible says that all the promises of God are yea and amen to them that believe (2 Corinthians 1:20). Notice that word *all*—all belief, all promises. Wow, that's big!

You see, when you have *all*, there isn't any more to be had. That means you've arrived! An elevated mind rises up to the level of your spirit. All you have to do is put down your flesh. It's called walking as God walks: in the Spirit!

Jesus—He'll Help You Keep It Simple

Now, to most Christians, walking in the Spirit is perplexing to the intellect. If it is to you too, remind yourself that your natural intellect can actually be used to make your faith in God better. You can use your mind to fight *for* faith instead of *against* faith. Use your intellect to fight for what is good and it will bring you closer to where you want to be. Remind yourself of what God has said and done.

Believe in the Wonderfulness of Jesus

When faith and belief come out of the spirit and mind, they confine themselves only to what God has said. Now, to many Christians, that kind of lifestyle is a whole other universe! But that is where God wants us to be—so full of faith in Him that our spirit and mind work together as one.

When I preach like this, some will say things like, "Well, I tried that, Brother Jesse, and it didn't work!" Well, when it comes to not getting results, the hard truth is this: The reason why some things "didn't work" is not because *Christ* failed in power, but because *we* as Christians so often fail in faith. Our motives can become complicated when we lose sight of the *simplicity* of faith and purpose.

Have you ever noticed that children never complicate faith? If you tell a kid that you will take them to Disney World in Orlando, Florida, they will run down the street telling everyone they meet, "I'm going to Disney World!" Why? Because they believe you! They take you at your word.

We are God's children; we are not God's adults! I just choose not to complicate faith and belief. And I make sure to make a demand on my faith by telling others what God said, too. It's important to stretch yourself in those areas—don't be afraid to let Jesus elevate your thinking and your speaking. When you step out in those areas, you elevate your life right along with your new thoughts and new words. God wants the BEST for you. Dare to want the best, too!

During Jesus' earthly life, they said of Him, *'Never has a Man spoke like this Man.' 'Who is this Man, that even the wind and the waves of the sea obey Him?'* (My paraphrase of John 7:46 and Mark 4:41.) And Isaiah, under divine prophecy, declared, *'His name shall be called Wonderful, Counsellor, the Mighty God, the Prince of Peace.'*

Discover the wonderfulness of Jesus for yourself. Ask Him to come into your heart and re-dress, re-establish, and revolutionize your life. Only Jesus can smooth away the rough edges of your life until you sparkle like a jewel in the sun. He is wonderful. BELIEVE!

CHAPTER 9
BELIEVE Your Vision, Receive Your Dreams

> *That Christ may dwell in your hearts by faith; that ye, being rooted and grounded in love,*
> *May be able to comprehend with all saints what is the breadth, and length, and depth, and height;*
> *And to know the love of Christ, which passeth knowledge, that ye might be filled with all the fulness of God.*
> *Now unto Him that is able to do exceeding abundantly above all that we ask or think, according to the power that worketh in us,*
> *Unto Him be glory in the church by Christ Jesus throughout all ages, world without end. Amen.*
> Ephesians 3:17-21

This is a powerful passage of scripture. First of all, it describes how Christ dwells in our hearts. It's *"by faith"* (v. 17). Why? Because love never fails. It goes on to say that we are to *"know"* the love of God (v. 19). Notice it doesn't say that we can just *believe* in the love of God. No, we are to really *know* that love—understand it by experiencing it and getting a revelation about it. Next, Paul said that the love of God *"passeth knowledge"* (v. 19). That means it is beyond our intellectual ability. God can give you peace when nothing but turmoil surrounds you. When peace seems like a pie in the sky, He can bring it down to where you are to a degree that you just don't understand—and nobody else understands either.

Paul continues to say in verse 19, *"...that ye might be filled with all the fulness of God"*—what higher dream could you have than to be filled with the fulness of God? That trumps everything because it affects everything. In God there is NO lack. No lack spiritually, no lack physically, no lack financially, or in any other way. The fullness of God is something you can have. It is not illegal, and you shouldn't make excuses for living lower than He wants. Just believe in Him and His Word. Know that He wants you to have it all!

I love verse 20: *"Now unto Him Who is able to do exceeding abundantly above all that we ask or think...."* It's strong. It sparks my imagination. It's like kid's stuff because kids have vivid imaginations. They can dream up all sorts of things and believe them, too. God doesn't want us to be *childish*, but He does want us to have *childlike faith*. Why? Because He *wants* to do exceeding abundantly above ALL that we can ask or think.

Now, it's not like He is going to drop it into our laps, though. If there is a pie in the sky, you will likely have to do something if you want to see it drop down so you can eat it. How do those dreams and things that we have only imagined actually happen? Only one way: *"...according to the power that worketh in us"* (v. 20). Notice you don't make it happen on your own, but you are most definitely involved. It's the "power" of God working in us that does the work. He works through YOU. So, it's a collaborative effort—part you, part God—that brings those dreams into reality and helps you accomplish out-of-the-box ideas and concepts.

It's a wonderful thing when you can actually have what you believe, what you think, what you ask…and enjoy it on earth. God wants us to go beyond just talking about His goodness; He wants us to see it come to pass in the little areas of life, as well as in the big areas. He is on our side.

In Earth as in Heaven

I don't want to miss a single thing God has for me, whether in Heaven or on earth. For centuries religion has tried to make us believe that we have to wait until we die to get what God has prepared for us. Sure, we'll have to wait for some things, like casting our crowns at Jesus' feet and taking possession of our mansion in Heaven. But I believe that He wants to fulfill His "Our Father" prayer in your life so that you can live out God's will *"in earth, as it is in Heaven"* (Matthew 6:10). That's a pretty tall order. You could say it is impossible, a dream, a totally out-of-the-box way of thinking. Guess what? That's why you can do it! If you could do things like that on your own, you wouldn't need God. He is Who makes the impossible possible. But you must get close to Him and allow Him to rip off those man-made mental limitations. That is what renewing your mind to the Word is all about. It's about changing the way you perceive things so that you can believe differently, and then have faith for something extraordinary.

Maybe you've lived in lack all your life but you want to live prosperously—in some *"in earth, as it is in Heaven"* kind of way. Guess what? You most certainly can do it. Plenty of believers around the world have fulfilled their dreams, even with what seemed like great limitations. Why should you be any different? Each of us has something that stands in our way or threatens to hold us back, but with God's Word, faith in Him, and faith in your dream, you can do anything. God can give you insights, concepts, and ideas that will empower you to do something good on the earth and be blessed as a result.

Of course, if you just spend all your time criticizing those who have succeeded and have more than you do, you'll never realize your dreams. You will never gain true prosperity. The bottom line is that you must change your *perception* of prosperity if you want prosperity—and I'm not just talking about money. Prosperity is a "whole self" teaching. In fact, you can be rich and still not be prosperous. It's about your spirit, your body, your mind, and your money. So, don't get the wrong idea: Heaven isn't just a bunch of mansions with people fighting in their front yards! No, there is peace there. There is joy there. There is no lack. But, yes, there are mansions!

Jesus said in John 14:2, *"In My Father's house are many mansions...."* I believe that the Lord has no problem with you having a mansion here because He has no problem with you having one there.

When Belief and Unbelief Meet, There Will Be War

It is unnatural to be without faith and belief—they are the pulse of the world. Even people who claim to be faithless have faith in something, and often in many things. They have faith that the sun will rise, and that they will wake up, they will work or not work, eat, etc. They have faith in people they don't know who claim God is dead. They have all sorts of faith and belief that they tap into daily, yet it brings them nowhere near the inner peace, strength, hope, or love that they could experience if they were to put their faith in something much greater than themselves or this temporal world.

Faith and belief really do keep the world of humanity going around. As a believer in the everlasting God—the Alpha and the Omega, the beginning and the end—you are fixing your faith on pure reliability because what He *said*, He will *do*. Whether you understand it all yet is irrelevant to the reality that He is God—He's the first and the last, and everything in between wouldn't be here without Him. If His Son, Jesus, tells you that your belief has the power to make "all things possible," then you can stake eternity on it that it does! Faith is the currency of God.

The only thing that can stop you, then, is when you turn your belief into unbelief. That little "un" causes a lot of problems. And it is really sad to say, but when faith and unbelief meet, there will be an internal tug of war. Yet, so often, faith and unbelief can be found within the same heart. The inner wars of mankind cause a lot of chaos.

In science, they call it matter and antimatter. They annihilate each other when they come together. That's why I hate unbelief disguised as belief. If you paint a picture of a great fire, I promise you, it will not burn! Did you get that? Don't pretend. Just choose to believe what Jesus says and it *will* work all the time. Remind yourself that Jesus says the same things all the time because He's the same yesterday, today, and forever. He's not changing!

Have Vision—Hear the Voice of Jesus

There is an economy and an order in the Kingdom of God. There is nothing required of mankind that is not also required of God. It is because God is perfect that we are required to work toward perfection—and the manifestations of Christ within our own life are one way in which two extremes meet.

In life, it seems that we cannot always enjoy the higher views in their cleanness, purity, and brilliance. But when we have vision and hear the voice of Jesus in the Word saying, *"If you can believe,"* our inner man's faith rises up, and that's all the revelation of divine majesty we need! Now, that's what motivates me.

A person once asked me, "Brother Jesse, why do you study the Bible so much?" I said very clearly to him, "So I can obey it!" I love the scripture in Isaiah where it says, *"If you are willing and obedient, you will eat the good of the land"* (Isaiah 1:19). Now, *that's* a revelation that can change your situation! Notice it didn't say you have to be sad, deprived, and disgusted—it said you have to be willing and obedient to God.

God has promised to do the hard work; all you have to do is just believe. Be *willing* to believe. Fight *for* your own faith; don't fight *against* yourself. Make peace with *obedience* to God knowing that His Word to you was written with extreme love and pure concern for *your* soul and *your* life. There is never a need to rebel against that kind of love, and there is no reason not to obey a Father Who feels such love and goodness towards you. Remind yourself that being willing and obedient is a form of humility to the One Who made it all. It's the secret to receiving the vision that God gave you. All you have to do is BELIEVE.

CHAPTER 10
Success Is Believing God

God wants the best for you, and every day is a new opportunity to put the past behind you and move forward. Success is about more than just getting ahead in life. It's about having a mission, moving toward your destiny, and arriving at particular destinations in your life. The Holy Spirit can lead you directly so you'll know *what* to do, *when* to do it, *where* to do it, and *how* to do it in anything you choose.

You know, if you take a look around the world, you'll find leaders and people everywhere who are at a loss about what to do. But we, as Christians, have a Higher Source available to us Who can guide us every day. We can show the world what successfully walking by faith means. And we'll do it in everything we set our hands to do (Deuteronomy 28:8).

Know That God Can't Lie

In 2 Timothy 1:12, Paul wrote to Timothy and said, *"For this reason I also suffer these things; nevertheless I am not ashamed, for I know Whom I have believed and am persuaded that He is able to keep what I have committed to Him until that Day"* (NKJV).

I want you to notice that Paul told Timothy that he *believed*—he used the word *believe* in past tense. So, he wasn't *trying* to believe. He was *certain* when it came to His faith in Jesus Christ.

Personally, when I received the revelation that God can't lie, it revolutionized my thinking. The Word of God exploded in my spirit. All the impossible things I thought this ministry couldn't do became possible. I saw things in a totally different way. Actually, the time that it usually took to do things sped up. I didn't have to wait long for my prayers to be answered. Isn't that wonderful?!

You see, belief is not a mental attitude but a moral appropriation. Faith helps us to take exclusive possession of the Word. It becomes more than words on a page. It becomes the directive for our lives. To live the abundant life Jesus promised us is a moral thing. It is our duty to excel for Christ's sake. Now, that's about more than just believing right.

The Gospel we believe is not just a divine book, but it is a divine man named Jesus Who was literally God in flesh form. You see, God is one with Christ, and He is one with His Word. John 1:1 tells us, *"In the beginning was the Word, and the Word was with God, and the Word was God."* So, when we speak about the Word, we are talking about a *Person*, and that is why it has the potential to change our life. God wants us to succeed in anything we set our hands to do. It will be Jesus—living in us and through us each day—that will bring us to a place of excellence in life. Now, that ought to make you shout!

Be a Person of Strong Conviction

In *The Amplified Bible, Classic Edition* of Isaiah 12:5, it says, *"Sing praises to the Lord, for He has done excellent things [gloriously]; let this be made known to all the earth."* The whole world needs to know that God can't lie. He is a doer of excellent things!

Convictions will lead you to accomplish your mission. They show you your destiny and get you to your destination.

In *The Amplified Bible, Classic Edition* of 1 Corinthians 4:20, it says, *"For the kingdom of God consists of and is based on not talk but power (moral power and excellence of soul)."* Now, that's conviction! When God sets convictions in you, they never change—they guide you via your heart's promptings. That's why they are so distinct and why you are confident when you don't stray from them. My ministry has never changed its original course. Why? Because God set the course of this ministry and my life. I'm confident in that. The convictions He placed within me all those years ago remain distinct to this day. In other words, God doesn't change, and neither do I.

Be a Well-Disciplined Thinker

Your whole spiritual fortune must be invested in this way of life, and that includes your thought life. Proverbs 23:7 says, *"For as he thinketh in his heart, so is he…."* So, what you *think* is what you will *become*. It is just the way God created us. This is why if you want to see your faith work, your mind must be a reservoir for God's revelations instead of a sewage pit of satanic thoughts. When your brain is filled with God's revelations instead of the devil's distractions, you will be confident in the heat of life. I know life is not easy, but it's a precious gift given to you.

People today are searching for fulfillment in all the wrong places, but as Mark 8:36 says, *"For what shall it profit a man, if he shall gain the whole world, and lose his own soul?"* This is why I am determined to share God's message every chance I get. I want to see people come to the knowledge of Jesus and see them healthy, blessed, and doing well.

When the apostle Paul said in 2 Timothy 1:12, *"For the which cause I also suffer these things: nevertheless I am not ashamed: for I know Whom I have believed, and am persuaded that He is able to keep that which I have committed unto Him against that day,"* I want you to notice those words *know*, *believed*, *persuaded*, and *committed* reveal ever-increasing degrees of growth. To thrive in our faith-walk, we must grow! Earlier I talked about how Paul used the word *believed*, the past tense of "believe." Now I want to focus on the word *know*.

A Knowing Faith

When you know something, you have passed the point of mere belief. *Knowing* is the foundation of faith through knowledge. The reason I live by faith is because I *know* it works. Years ago, I heard Oral Roberts say that we need to "know it in our knower." Now, I don't know if that's correct English, but it sure went off in my spirit.

Faith always works if you work it. I *know* that. I think the reason some people don't know "in Whom they have believed" is because they try to live on *someone else's* faith. They haven't developed faith for themselves. They haven't investigated their own faith.

An uninvestigated faith is an unhappy faith. When you have uninvestigated and unhappy faith, you don't believe what you hear God *say*. Instead, you simply go by what you *see*, and that's a disaster waiting to happen. When you walk in "knowing faith," it works because it rests upon a person and not a doctrine.

To me, a *knowing* faith is Jesus Christ personified. I know that Jesus will do what He *said*, what He *says*, and what He's *going to say*. My whole life in Christ is based upon Him. Even the Father based everything on Jesus. That's why the apostle Paul said, *"For I know Whom I have believed."* Glory!

Rise Above the Language of Hesitation

The body of Christ must rise higher than mental intelligence… we must walk in revelation knowledge. It is the key to knowing Him the way our Father knows Him. We must rise above the language of *hesitation*.

I will not hesitate when God tells me to do something. If Satan tries to make me sick, I *immediately* speak, "By Jesus' stripes, I am healed." When God tells me to give a word of prophecy to someone, I *immediately* do it. You see, that's rising above the language of hesitation.

Some people have lost the battle because they hesitated a little. But when you *know*, it propels you to press toward the end result. The Word says, *"I press toward the mark for the prize of the high calling of God in Christ Jesus"* (Philippians 3:14). We have a prize to get, both you and I, and we will get there. Just BELIEVE!

CHAPTER 11
The Assurance of Knowing

Without experience in *knowing*, we cannot have assurance. Doubt has no room when experience and assurance are your track record. I told you that I've convinced myself that God can't lie. What makes me say that? Well, I have experience and I have assurance regarding His purity. Doubt doesn't have a chance in that environment. Doubt is destroyed by *knowing*—and experience and assurance bury it forever.

God can be trusted. Numbers 23:19 says, *"God is not a man, that He should lie; neither the son of man, that He should repent: hath He said, and shall He not do it? or hath He spoken, and shall He not make it good?"*

Scriptures like that build your *knowing*. They confirm your faith in His purity. Then your knowing will end up giving you more and more experiences of God's faithfulness. You'll have testimonies to share with others. It's time for you to forget where you buried your doubt once and for all because you will never go back and dig it up again!

Being Fully Persuaded

Now that we have gone over the first two specific words that Paul spoke in 2 Timothy 1:12, *believing* and *knowing*, I want to focus on the word *persuaded*.

Being fully *persuaded* about God's Word is what makes you *great* all over. It means you are going far beyond the average believer and anything is possible for you.

Persuaded means you've made up your mind, and nothing that happens can change your faith. Let me give you an example.

The Assurance of Knowing

When Jesus hung on the cross, He was so persuaded that what He was doing was right, He prayed, *"Father, forgive them; for they know not what they do"* (Luke 23:34). Now, that is persuaded!

Jesus *knew* that He had to take on the sins of the world so that we could come back into relationship with the Father. He was fully persuaded. His choice to hang on the cross was, is, and forever will be the greatest act of love toward mankind. It was a gift, paid for in His sinless blood. No other religious leader has ever done that.

Love Never Fails

Christ knew that love never fails (1 Corinthians 13:8). And because He was persuaded that God's plan of redemption was His death on the cross and resurrection from the dead, He was able to extend a love that was so powerful, it brought Him to the point of sacrifice and He cancelled *all* failure on our part. Now, that ought to make you shout!

You are someone going somewhere to succeed. I'm persuaded of that wholeheartedly! The reason I know it is because of Christ's sacrifice that has given you the ability to succeed—spiritually, physically, financially, and in every other way.

It's Personal—And It's a Key to Overcoming

Your full persuasion didn't come from just thoughtlessly doing what you were told to do. Your faith became a *personal* act of love toward God and *His* holy instruction—something very important to you.

The purest actions are those that abandon human understanding in favor of God's divine truth—it's your childlike trust in God's divine inspiration and instruction on full display. Being fully *persuaded* makes you very keen on what God is saying.

> *You are of God, little children, and have overcome them, because He Who is in you is greater than he who is in the world.*
>
> 1 John 4:4 NKJV

BELIEVE

You can overcome anything because Jesus, the Greater One, lives in you. When you get fully persuaded that you have the power to overcome, it's going to get you excited! That's why there is hardly a word in the Bible more encouraging, stimulating, assuring, and worth remembering than the word *persuaded*—it changes your mindset from victim to victor when you know that the Greater One lives in *YOU!*

Your Answer Is Older Than Your Problem

The Person we serve was here before Satan and his cohorts. Did you know that all God's answers are older than all the problems Satan throws at you? Jesus is so far ahead of the devil concerning your life! Go and read Matthew 6:25-34 and remember that's why Jesus said over and over, *"Take no thought."* Why? Because He doesn't want you to worry. Seek first the Kingdom because *that's* what fully persuaded people do!

I love that, *"Take no thought."* I like the way the Italians say it: "Fuhgeddaboudit!" (That's "forget about it," ha ha!) The answers God has given you are just that good! They are trustworthy, and that's why it's important to be fully persuaded that what God said *is* true and *will* come to pass for those who believe. Remember, we are spiritual athletes, not spiritual invalids!

Necessary Truth Grows on Low Branches

As a believer, you don't have to reach high for your answers in life because all the necessary truth you need grows on low branches. In other words, God made it easy for us to reach what we need. I could also say it this way: God is never out of *your* reach, and you are never out of *His* reach. That is the miracle of redemption. Christ closed the gap through an act of fully-persuaded love.

Even a baby Christian can feed himself. It may be a little sloppy, but food will get into his mouth! In Romans 4:21-22, the Word talks about how Abraham's faith gave him righteousness (right standing with God) in a time before the cross. *"And being fully persuaded that, what He had promised, He was able also to per-*

form. And therefore it was imputed to him for righteousness." That's how serious God takes being fully persuaded! Abraham was fully persuaded about the promises of God and He became the father of our faith.

I want you to remember that Abraham didn't start out fully persuaded. He didn't start there, but he got there…and you will, too!

Committed Is a Divine Transaction

Now I want to zero in on the word *committed* in 2 Timothy 1:12, *"…For I know Whom I have believed, and am persuaded that He is able to keep that which I have <u>committed</u> unto Him against that day."*

Committed is a powerful word. To me, it means you are determined to get the job done. Some people are afraid of the word *committed*, but what I like about commitment is that it gets results. When you commit something to God, it becomes a divine transaction—unbreakable and unalterable.

God has promised to be faithful to His Word. When you commit something to God, you are agreeing that you, too, will keep your word. He is keeping His Word to you and you are keeping your word to Him—and as I just mentioned, that becomes an unbreakable and unalterable divine transaction. When you choose to become committed, power begins to manifest. Faith draws it out and things begin to change in life.

Committed Brings Out the Best in You

I made up my mind when I went into full-time ministry in 1976 that I would not falter or fail in the work of the Lord. It's important to me and the kingdom of God that I do not falter or fail in doing what He has called me to do. You see, the word *committed* holds my feet to the fire! When you are committed, it will hold your feet to the fire, too, but it will also bring out the *best* in you. It pushes you to do more and believe more, and it is inspiring to others as well.

Your choice to commit something to God gives Him bragging rights! God loves to brag on His children. He loves it when we trust and put our faith in Him. He loves it when we obey His Word because He knows that it will bring out the very best in us. There is no better way than God's way.

Committed Produces Healthy Words

When you commit something to God, it also produces sound words—and sound words are healthy words. Healthy words are the outcome of a healthy heart.

In Matthew 12:35 it says, *"A good man out of the good treasure of the heart bringeth forth good things: and an evil man out of the evil treasure bringeth forth evil things."* So, according to that verse, being committed will produce either good or evil. I would prefer the good, wouldn't you?

Committed Produces Doers, Not Tryers

I've heard people say, "Brother Jesse, I'm trying to get this to work!" I often say, "Now, that's the problem!" Commitment doesn't *try*. Commitment gets the job done! God can't keep what you won't *commit* to Him.

It is what you determine to *do* that matters most. When you determine to have faith in God and commit things to Him, you are allowing Him to show Himself strong on your behalf and honor His Word. But if you don't commit anything, how can you expect to get anything?

God isn't motivated by your *need*; He is motivated by your *faith*. Look in the Word and you will see that for yourself. You see, the Word won't work for a person who doesn't believe or apply it! That's why there is such an important difference between *committing* something to God and just *trying* to get things to work.

Committed Is a Way Out of Frustration

Trying will produce frustration, while *doing* will produce what you believe for. You see, when you *try* to do something, your whole heart and mind are not really into it. By even saying, "I'm trying," you are already making a provision for failure.

The Assurance of Knowing

If you *try* to go on a diet, you will break it. But if you make up your heart and mind and you tell yourself, "I'm going to do this no matter how hungry I get," you are going to lose weight. The world is full of *tryers*. God calls us to be *doers*. In other words, I remove the *try* out of my mind. I'm determined that whatever I *commit* to the Lord, He is fully and completely able to do.

Committed Doesn't Live at Random

Commitment is always founded upon trust. So, the more you *know* the Lord, the more you will trust Him and commit to Him. This is why it is so important to develop a daily habit of fellowshipping with God. Put Him first. Refuse to live at random.

I do *not* live at random. My commitment to God is important to me—it's not insignificant. I say what the apostle Paul said: "*…He is able to keep that which I have committed unto Him against that day.*"

I believe that commitment is what made the apostle Paul the great man that he was. Even when he was a "chief of sinners," as he called himself, he was committed to his work of destroying Christianity. But on that road to Damascus, God changed his zeal for hurting people into a zeal for helping people receive Christ. What a transformation!

You see, that's what happened to me. Before I was saved, I was determined to live for the devil. I made up my mind that I would sin when I wanted to, how I wanted to, and as many times as I wanted to. But something happened to me on Labor Day weekend in 1974. In a bathroom in Boston, Massachusetts, I met the Lord Jesus Christ!

You may know the story, but, in short, I was about to go and play rock music. I was in a hotel room getting ready…and that's when I heard about the love of Christ. It was through a television set that I heard about Christ. And the love I heard about overwhelmed me to such a degree that I wanted to cry. And because I didn't want my wife, Cathy, to see me, I went into that hotel bathroom. There, I cried to God to save me, just as the man on television had said to do.

BELIEVE

What did I do? I committed. I committed my life to Him—I asked Him to come into my heart and save me. I committed my body—that from then on, I would be pure for Him. I committed my finances—that I would give to further the knowledge of Him. I committed my whole destiny and destination to Him—that His will would be done in my life.

How could I do that? Trust. A refusal to live at random. You see, I trusted in the God Who loved me enough to send His only begotten Son, and so, because I trusted in His love, it was easy to commit my life to Him.

Committed Really Is the Only Way to Live

After that critical moment in my life, all I can tell you is this…I understand Paul's words: *"For I know Whom I have believed, and am persuaded that He is able to keep that which I have <u>committed</u> unto Him against that day."* God kept His promise to save me. All I had to do was meet the condition and call upon His name.

Guess what? Today, *I'm* "the man on television!" Today, people all over the world are doing just what I did back in 1974 in that hotel room in Boston, Massachusetts. They are tuning in and hearing about the love and power of Jesus, and the Holy Spirit is drawing them to salvation. Glory! Salvation is for everyone. Today, I am so blessed to be on the other side of the salvation prayer—sharing my Jesus with the world and giving exactly what I was given: an opportunity to meet the Lord and get committed. To me, *committed* really is the only way to live. Only Jesus can lead us out of darkness and into His glorious light—when we BELIEVE.

PRAYER OF SALVATION

A born-again, committed relationship with God is the key to a victorious life. Jesus, the Son of God, laid down His life and rose again so that we could spend eternity with Him in Heaven and experience His absolute best here on earth. The Bible says, *"For God so loved the world, that He gave His only begotten Son, that whosoever believeth in Him should not perish, but have everlasting life"* (John 3:16).

It is the will of God that everyone receives eternal salvation. The way to receive this salvation is to call upon the name of Jesus and confess Him as your Lord. The Bible also tells us, *"That if thou shalt confess with thy mouth the Lord Jesus, and shalt believe in thine heart that God hath raised Him from the dead, thou shalt be saved…For whosoever shall call upon the name of the Lord shall be saved"* (Romans 10:9,13).

Jesus has given salvation, healing, and countless benefits to all who call upon His name. These benefits can be yours if you receive Him into your heart by praying this prayer:

> *Heavenly Father, I come to You admitting that I am a sinner. Right now, I choose to turn away from sin, and I ask You to cleanse me of all unrighteousness. I believe that Your Son, Jesus, died on the cross to take away my sins. I also believe that He rose again from the dead so that I may be justified and made righteous through faith in Him. I call upon the name of Jesus Christ to be the Savior and Lord of my life. Jesus, I choose to follow You, and I ask that You fill me with the power of the Holy Spirit. Right now, I declare that I am a born-again child of God. I am free from sin and full of the righteousness of God. I am saved in Jesus' name. Amen.*

If you have prayed this prayer to receive Jesus Christ as your Savior, or if this book has been a blessing to you, we would like to hear from you. Please contact us at:

Jesse Duplantis Ministries
PO Box 1089
Destrehan, LA 70047
985.764.2000
www.jdm.org

ABOUT THE AUTHOR

Jesse Duplantis, minister of the Gospel, motivational speaker, television personality, and best-selling author, has been in full-time ministry since 1976 and is the founder of Jesse Duplantis Ministries, located in the Greater New Orleans area of south Louisiana in the United States of America. With over four decades of sharing his unique blend of humor and faith around the world, generations of believers have been inspired by his messages, and countless numbers have come to know Jesus Christ as Savior through his ministry.

Known for his unflinching, status-quo-breaking messages, and humorous take on experiences in the life of the believer, Jesse continues to draw large audiences of believers through social media, television, and meetings held around the world. With speaking engagements booked years in advance, Jesse Duplantis continues to keep an intense traveling schedule, flying throughout the United States and the world preaching the Gospel of Jesus Christ. With no booking agents pursuing meetings for him and no set fees imposed upon churches for speaking engagements, Jesse chooses his outreach meetings based on the same two criteria he always has: invitations that come in and prayer over each one. This uncommon way of scheduling in today's world means Jesse's many followers may find him speaking in some of the largest churches and venues in America and the world, as well as a great many small and growing congregations, too. No church is too big or small for the Holy Spirit, as he says.

Side by side with his wife Cathy Duplantis, the co-founder and chief of staff of Jesse Duplantis Ministries and the senior pastor of Covenant Church in Destrehan, Louisiana, Jesse continues to fulfill his life's calling by daily taking up the Great Commission of Jesus Christ: *"Go ye into all the world, and preach the Gospel to every creature"* (Mark 16:15). Through social media, television broadcasts, books, and other ministry products, as well as through many evangelistic meetings, the JDM website, the JDM App, and *Voice of the Covenant* magazine, Jesse Duplantis continues to see growth in his ministry and expand each year while maintaining his roots. Jesus is the center of his life. The salvation of lost people and the growth of believers is the purpose of his ministry. And for both he and his wife, every day is another day to "Reach People and Change Lives, One Soul at a Time."

Other Books by Jesse Duplantis

The Hidden Help**
The Mysterious Work of Angels in the Bible and in My Life

I Never Learned to Doubt
Lessons I've Learned About the Dangers of Doubt and the Freedom of Faith

The Most Wonderful Time of the Year
Uncommon Lessons from the Christmas Story

Your Everything Is His Anything
Expand Your View of What Prayer and Faith Can Do

Advance in Life
From Revelation to Inspiration to Manifestation

The Big 12
My Personal Confidence-Building Principles for Achieving Total Success

Living at the Top
How to Prosper God's Way and Avoid the Pitfalls of Success

For by IT…FAITH
If You Don't Know What "IT" Is, You Won't Have It!

Distortion
The Vanity of Genetically Altered Christianity

The Everyday Visionary
Focus Your Thoughts, Change Your Life

What in Hell Do You Want?

Wanting a God You Can Talk To**

Jambalaya for the Soul
Humorous Stories and Cajun Recipes from the Bayou

Breaking the Power of Natural Law
Finding Freedom in the Presence of God

God Is Not Enough, He's Too Much!
How God's Abundant Nature Can Revolutionize Your Life

Heaven: Close Encounters of the God Kind**

The Ministry of Cheerfulness

*** Also Available in Spanish*

OTHER CONTENT:
Other ministry resources by Jesse Duplantis are available through
jdm.org and the JDM App

CONTACT US

To contact Jesse Duplantis Ministries with prayer requests, praise reports, comments, or to schedule Jesse Duplantis at your church, conference, or seminar, please write, call, or email:

Jesse Duplantis Ministries
PO Box 1089
Destrehan, LA 70047
985-764-2000
www.jdm.org

We also invite you to connect with us on social media:

Facebook:	/JesseDuplantisMinistries
X:	@jesse_duplantis
Instagram:	@jesseduplantisministries
YouTube:	/jesseduplantisministries
Pinterest:	/JesseDuplantisMinistries
TikTok:	@jesseduplantisministries
Rumble:	/JesseDuplantisMinistries